Safety and health
in dock work

ILO Codes of Practice

Safety and health in dock work

Revised edition

International Labour Office Geneva

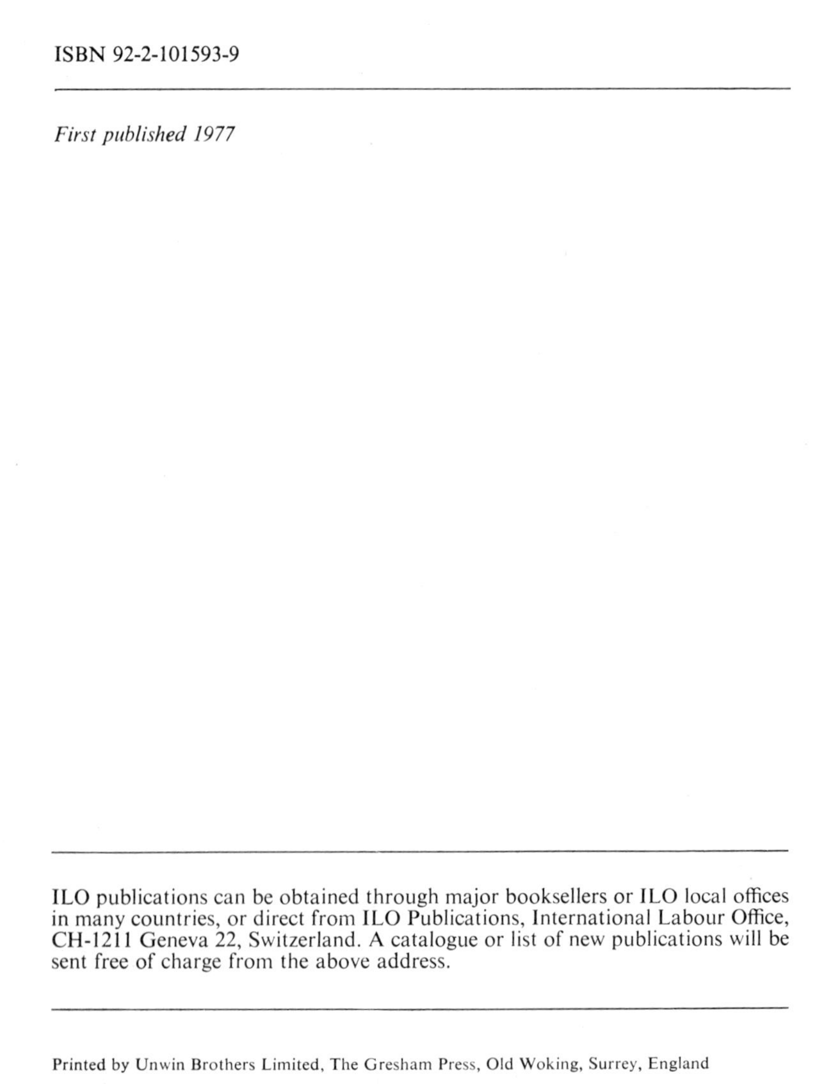

ISBN 92-2-101593-9

First published 1977

ILO publications can be obtained through major booksellers or ILO local offices in many countries, or direct from ILO Publications, International Labour Office, CH-1211 Geneva 22, Switzerland. A catalogue or list of new publications will be sent free of charge from the above address.

Printed by Unwin Brothers Limited, The Gresham Press, Old Woking, Surrey, England

Preface

There has been a substantial increase in transport by sea and by inland waterway over the past three decades: the amount of dry cargo loaded and unloaded in maritime ports throughout the world increased from some 375 million tonnes in 1937 to over 1,000 million tonnes in the early 1970s. When the first edition of the ILO code of practice relating to safety and health in dock work was prepared, it was based on the most usual pattern of dock work at the time, namely the "break-bulk" system under which cargo was largely handled piecemeal with the aid of dockside cranes, ship's gear and normal road transport. Goods were laboriously made up in sets in the 'tween decks or on the dockside and lifted by means of slings, cargo nets or pallets. Lifts of over 5 tonnes were the exception rather than the rule. The work involved was both arduous and dangerous, and as a result this occupation had one of the highest accident frequency and severity rates.

While dock work continues to follow this pattern in many parts of the world, there have been some highly significant developments that are leading to profound changes in the nature of the work. Perhaps the most spectacular of these changes has been the introduction of freight containers; with their aid a ship of 30,000 tonnes or more can be turned round in two or three days, during which time 2,000 or more containers may have been handled. A second development has been the introduction of the "Ro-Ro" system—roll-on-roll-off ships by means of which large quantities of freight travels from country to country on lorries without unloading. To meet these developments, a number of new ocean terminals have been designed and laid out to handle this traffic exclusively. Sophisticated mobile lifting equipment has been introduced, and mechanically operated loading doors, ramps and lifts are to be found in the ships themselves, enabling powered fork-lift trucks and similar vehicles to move goods from deck to deck and from ship to shore.

This situation led the Governing Body of the International Labour Office to convene a meeting of experts on safety and health in dock work, which was held in January 1976. The meeting was attended by three experts appointed after consultations with governments, three experts appointed after consultations with the Employers' members and three experts appointed after consultations with the Workers' members of the Governing Body.[1] The second item on the agenda of the meeting was the revision of the ILO code of practice on safety and health in dock work. The experts agreed to incorporate in the code a number of new provisions, and to revise some of the existing ones.

As in the case of the first edition, the present revised code of practice is intended not as a set of regulations but as a guide consisting of a body of concise recommendations supplemented by a number of appendices relating to the testing of lifting appliances and other items. At the meeting the experts stressed that while they welcomed the opportunity of revising the code in view of the technological developments that had taken place in this field, there were

---

[1] The nine experts were:

Mr. T. Cronin, National Secretary, Docks Group, Transport and General Workers' Union, London.

Mr. G. A. Cullington, Managing Director, Hull and Humber Cargo Handling Co. Ltd., Hull.

Mr. Sergio Dahmen Carvacho, Chief of the Maritime Section of the Division of Prevention of Occupational Hazards, Occupational Safety Institute, Viña del Mar.

Mr. J. K. Enimpah, Safety and Training Officer, Tema Shipyard and Drydock Corporation, Tema.

Mr. C. H. Fitzgibbon, General Secretary, Waterside Workers' Federation of Australia, Sydney.

Mr. T. W. Gleason, International President, International Longshoremen's Association, New York.

Captain E. C. March, US Department of Labor, Occupational Safety and Health Administration, Washington, DC.

Mr. M. J. McEntee, HM Engineering Inspector of Factories, Health and Safety Executive, London.

Mr. T. N. Novikov, Deputy Head, Labour Regulations and Wage Policy Department, Ministry of Merchant Marine, Moscow.

In addition the following international governmental and non-governmental organisations sent representatives to the meeting:

— World Health Organization
— Inter-Governmental Maritime Consultative Organisation
— International Organisation for Standardisation.

many provisions of the existing code that were still valid in view of the fact that a large proportion of break-bulk cargo was still handled by conventional methods in many parts of the world. They were aware that not all the provisions of the revised code could be applied as they stood to all countries or to all regions, and that there would be a need in some cases for provisions to be adapted to local conditions.

They also recognised that it would be difficult to apply some of the recommendations to existing equipment, whereas there would be no such problem in the case of equipment that was newly introduced. It was their opinion, therefore, that existing equipment that was not in conformity with the provisions of the revised code should wherever practicable be brought into compliance as soon as possible, for example during a major refit. New equipment should satisfy the new requirements.

A further point made by the experts was that the relevant provisions of the revised code should be applicable to LASH or similar systems under which barges are carried aboard large vessels, although no specific reference to such systems appeared in the revised code.

In conclusion, the experts considered that the revised code constituted a body of advice which ILO member States were likely to find of great value. It could provide useful guidance for all bodies and persons concerned with safety and health in dock work, such as government authorities, employers and workers, manufacturers of equipment, and professional bodies dealing with occupational safety and health.

Valuable assistance in the preparation of the revised code was given to the Office by Mr. R. A. Stockbridge, CEng, FIMechE, FRINA, of the United Kingdom.

Contents

1. General provisions

1.1. Definitions

1.1.1. For the purposes of this code, unless otherwise noted—

(*a*) "dock work" means and includes all or any part of the work, or those duties associated with the work, performed on shore or on board ship, of loading or unloading any ship whether engaged in maritime or inland navigation, excluding ships of war, in, on or at any maritime or inland port, harbour, dock, wharf, quay or similar place at which such work is carried on;

(*b*) the "coefficient of utilisation" (formerly known as the "factor of safety") is the numerical value obtained by dividing the minimum breaking load or tension of an item of equipment by its certified safe working load;

(*c*) the "competent authority" is a minister, government department or other authority empowered to issue regulations, orders, or other instructions having the force of law;

(*d*) a "competent person" is a person who has been approved as qualified by training or experience to perform a task or function or assume a responsibility in a manner that will prevent danger as far as is practicable;

(*e*) "flameproof" or "explosion-proof" denotes a method of construction such that explosions occurring within a machine or piece of electrical gear cannot be transmitted outside its enclosure;

(*f*) a "heavy lift derrick" is a ship's derrick that is specially rigged for use from time to time in order to lift weights greater than the safe working load of the ship's light or general purpose lift gear;

(*g*) an "intermodal container" is a rigid, rectangular, re-usable cargo container intended to contain bulk commodities or one or more articles of cargo for shipment aboard a vessel, and capable of utilisation for this purpose by one or more other means of transport without intermediate reloading; the term includes completely enclosed units, open-top units or other fractional height units, units incorporating liquid or gas tanks, and any other variations, whether demountable or with attached wheels, serving the same basic purpose and fitting into the container system; however, the term does not include cylinders, drums, crates, cases, cartons, packages, sacks, unitised loads or any other of the usual forms of packaging;

(*h*) a "ship's derrick crane" is a ship's derrick having a boom which may be raised, lowered and slewed transversely while supporting a load, by means of winches which either form an integral part of the arrangement or are used primarily with it;

(*i*) a "skeletal vehicle" is a chassis used to move intermodal containers, the longitudinal member of the chassis consisting of a centreline beam that is fitted at or near each end with a transverse member to which the wheels and corner fittings are attached;

(*j*) a "transporter" is a gantry-type, rail-mounted crane, equipped with a horizontal bridge from which is operated a trolley or trolleys used with such items of equipment as grabs, magnets and container spreaders; and

(*k*) a "vessel" is any ship, boat (other than a rowing boat), barge or floating construction such as a floating dock, a drilling platform or any similar floating structure.

1.2. Role of bodies and persons concerned with dock work

1.2.1. National regulations for the protection of dockworkers against accidents and injuries to health should clearly define the bodies and persons whose individual or joint duty it is to comply with the different provisions of those regulations.

1.2.2. Bodies and persons that own or control workplaces on ships or on dock premises where dock work is carried on, or provide plant and equipment for use in dock work, should provide and maintain such workplaces, plant and equipment in a safe condition.

1.2.3. Bodies and persons that employ dockworkers should—

(*a*) provide such supervision as will ensure that the conditions of work of dockworkers shall be as safe and healthy as possible;

(*b*) if not themselves the bodies and persons described in paragraph 1.2.2, co-operate with those bodies and persons in keeping workplaces and equipment safe;

(*c*) satisfy themselves that dockworkers are properly instructed in the hazards of their respective occupations and the precautions necessary to avoid accidents and injuries to health, and in particular that newly engaged dockworkers are properly instructed concerning hazards and precautions, and are adequately supervised; and

(*d*) ensure that dockworkers are fully informed in an appropriate manner of the contents of national or local regulations relating to the protection of dockworkers against accidents and injuries to health.

1.2.4. (1) Dockworkers should forthwith report to their foreman or employer, or if necessary to the competent authority, any defect that is apt to cause danger and that they may discover in workplaces or in plant and equipment used therein.

(2) If the defect is such as to cause immediate danger, the use of the workplaces, plant or equipment affected should not be permitted until the defect has been remedied.

1.2.5. Dockworkers should make proper use of all safeguards, safety devices and other appliances furnished for their protection or the protection of others.

1.2.6. Except in case of necessity, no dockworker, unless duly authorised, should interfere with, remove, alter or displace any safety device or other appliance furnished for his protection or the protection of others, or interfere with any method or process adopted with a view to avoiding accidents and injuries to health.

1.2.7. Dockworkers should make themselves acquainted with and obey all safety and health instructions pertaining to their work.

1.2.8. Dockworkers should refrain from careless or reckless

practices or actions that are likely to result in accidents or injuries to health.

1.2.9. All bodies and persons concerned with dock work should co-operate in carrying out all measures that will promote the safety and health of dockworkers, without prejudice to any obligation laid upon them by national regulations.

1.3. Housekeeping

1.3.1. All wharves, quays, decks and similar places where dock work is carried on should be kept adequately clear and, as far as practicable, free from objects that can cause slipping, falling or stumbling.

1.3.2. Warehouses, storeplaces, wharves, quays and decks where dock work is carried on should be kept clean and, as far as practicable, free from rubbish.

1.3.3. Loose gear, tools and similar equipment should be removed from working areas when not in use.

1.3.4. Running gear such as guy ends, preventers, bridles and pendants should be coiled in a workmanlike manner in the immediate vicinity of the fastening devices.

1.3.5. Places on shore, on board, on pontoons or on any means of access to ships that have to be used by dockworkers and have become slippery owing to rain, snow, ice, grease, oil or any other cause should, as far as practicable, be cleaned or made safe by strewing suitable material such as sand, ashes, sawdust or salt, or by other suitable means.

1.4. Dangers from work other than dock work

1.4.1. No other work, for example maintenance or repair work such as chipping, caulking, spray painting, sandblasting or welding, should be performed at places where dock work is in progress if it might endanger or obstruct the persons carrying out the dock work because of gases, fumes, dust, radiation, noise or any other nuisance.

1.5. Machinery

1.5.1. Unless their position or construction makes them as safe as they would be if securely guarded, all dangerous parts of machinery, motors, wheels, chain and friction gearing, shafting and steam pipes on board ship or on shore where dockworkers have to work or pass should be securely guarded so far as is practicable without impeding the safe working of ships.

1.5.2. The guarding of dangerous parts of machinery should not be removed while the machinery is in use, but if removed by an authorised person should be replaced as soon as practicable, and in any case before the machinery is taken into normal use again.

1.5.3. No machine part that is in motion and that is not securely guarded should be examined, lubricated, adjusted or repaired except by duly authorised persons.

1.5.4. Machine parts should be cleaned only when the machine is stopped.

1.5.5. When machinery is stopped for servicing or repairs, adequate measures should be taken to ensure that it cannot be inadvertently re-started.

1.5.6. Only duly authorised persons should be permitted to remove guarding from dangerous machinery.

1.6. Qualifications of winch and crane drivers, signallers, etc.

1.6.1. Only sufficiently competent and reliable persons should be employed to operate lifting or transporting machinery, whether driven by mechanical power or otherwise, to give signals to a driver of such machinery or to attend to cargo falls on winch ends or winch drums.

1.7. Duties of signallers

1.7.1. A signaller at a hatch should do his utmost to protect the gang working at his hatch against accidents.

1.7.2. Signallers should be stationed at a position where they can best follow the work.

1.7.3. A signaller's signals to a winch or crane driver should be distinct.

1.7.4. Signallers should when necessary warn persons in cargo holds, on lighters and ashore.

1.7.5. Before work is started for the day, a signaller should see that his workplace on the ship's deck or on the deck cargo is clear.

1.7.6. Before giving a signal to hoist, a signaller should see that the load is properly slung and that hoisting can be started without risk to persons working in the hold or on deck.

1.7.7. No signal to lower a load should be given by a signaller unless all is clear in the hold and the hatchway or, as the case may be, on the deck or in the lighter.

1.7.8. Before giving the signal to land, a signaller should satisfy himself that the load can be safely landed.

1.7.9. A signaller should see that no persons are carried by lifting appliances except by special authority.

1.8. Ventilation

1.8.1. In each compartment where cargo is worked, effective and suitable provision should be made for securing and maintaining adequate ventilation of the compartment by the circulation of fresh air.

1.9. Lighting

1.9.1. All places on shore or on board where dock work is carried on, all approaches and means of access to such places, and all places to which dockworkers may be required to proceed in the course of their work, should be efficiently lighted, so long as any dockworkers are present, whenever natural lighting is inadequate.

1.9.2. The means of lighting should not endanger the health or safety of dockworkers, or the safety of the ship, the cargo or the navigation of other vessels.

1.9.3. The general illumination in areas on docks, wharves and quays where dockworkers have to pass should be at least 5 lux (0.5 foot-candle).

1.9.4. At places ashore where loading or unloading and related operations are in progress, the illumination should be at least 20 lux (2 foot-candles).

1.9.5. At places where loading or unloading operations are in progress on board ships and lighters, such illumination as is reasonably practicable should be provided; this illumination should be at least 20 lux (2 foot-candles).

1.9.6. The illumination of all other parts of a vessel over which persons employed in the operations have to pass should not be less than 8 lux (0.8 foot-candles).

1.9.7. The requirements mentioned in paragraphs 1.9.3 to 1.9.6 refer to illumination in the horizontal plane at a height of 1 m above the working surface.

1.9.8. (1) The requirements referred to in paragraphs 1.9.3 to 1.9.6 apply primarily to general cargo working, and should serve as a guide in the planning of new lighting installations.

(2) These standards should be without prejudice to the provision of any additional illumination at particularly dangerous places, for example at shore gangways, accommodation ladders and breaks in quays.

1.9.9. The means of artificial lighting should be such as to maintain a reasonable uniformity and constancy of illumination; so far as is reasonably practicable they should be such, or be so arranged, as to reduce glare and dazzle to a minimum and prevent the formation of shadows that might conceal a danger.

1.9.10. Persons passing from one area to another should not, so far as is practicable, be subjected suddenly to sharp contrasts in levels of illumination.

1.10. Electrical equipment

1.10.1. (1) All electrical equipment and circuits used in dock work should be so designed, constructed, installed, protected and maintained as to prevent danger in accordance with the requirements of national regulations and of the competent authority.

(2) Where such requirements do not exist, reference should be made to relevant provisions of the *Model Code of Safety Regulations for Industrial Establishments for the Guidance of Governments and Industry*.[1]

1.10.2. Only duly authorised persons should be permitted to install, adjust, examine, repair, displace or remove electrical equipment or circuits.

1.10.3. Efficient and suitably located means should be provided for cutting off all electrical current from every part of the system as may be necessary to prevent danger.

1.10.4. All portable electrical equipment should be inspected by a competent person at least once in every day of use.

1.10.5. Electrical equipment for use in places where there is an explosion risk should be of a suitable flameproof type for the atmosphere in question.

1.10.6. Electrical equipment exposed to the weather should be adequately protected against wet or corrosion.

1.10.7. All non-current-carrying metal parts of electrical equipment should be earthed, or other suitable measures should be taken to prevent them from becoming live.

1.10.8. Portable or flexible electric conductors should be kept clear of loads, running gear and moving equipment.

1.10.9. Portable electric lamps should be used only—

(*a*) where adequate permanent fixed lighting cannot be provided; and

(*b*) at a voltage safe in the particular conditions of work.

---

[1] Published by the International Labour Office.

1.11. Hand tools

1.11.1. Hand tools should be of good material and construction, and maintained in safe condition.

1.11.2. Hand tools should be periodically inspected by a competent person, and defective tools should be immediately replaced or repaired.

1.12. Fire protection

1.12.1. Places where dockworkers are employed should if necessary be provided with—

(*a*) sufficient and suitable fire-extinguishing equipment; and

(*b*) an adequate water supply at ample pressure.

1.12.2. Persons trained to use the fire-extinguishing equipment should be readily available during all working periods.

1.12.3. Fire-extinguishing equipment should be properly maintained, and inspected at suitable intervals.

1.12.4. Rules concerning the places and times at which smoking may be permitted should be laid down by the appropriate authority according to circumstances.

1.12.5. Adequate and safe means of escape in case of fire should be provided, as well as an adequate fire alarm system where necessary.

1.12.6. The responsible authority should make arrangements for the regular inspection of processes and premises to seek out fire hazards.

1.12.7. Dockworkers should be advised of the cases where it is dangerous or not advisable to use water to extinguish fires.

2. Docks

2.1. Surface

2.1.1. Any regular approach over a dock should be maintained with due regard to the safety of persons and equipment used by dockworkers.

2.1.2. The surface should be—

(*a*) properly drained to remove rainwater so far as is practicable;

(*b*) kept free from any depressions or holes and raised parts such as kerbs apt to be a danger to any person or to any vehicle or lifting appliance;

(*c*) of adequate strength for the wheel loading of any vehicle or lifting appliance where such vehicles or appliances are used or apt to be used;

(*d*) as level as is reasonably practicable;

(*e*) kept free, so far as is reasonably practicable, of any substance apt to make a foothold insecure or to impair the handling of any mechanical equipment.

2.1.3. Any part of the dock surface that is under repair should be suitably barricaded or flagged off, and provided with a flashing warning or other suitable light if the dock is used at night.

2.1.4. Any ramp or slope that is used by, or apt to be used by, a fork-lift truck or other vehicle the safety of which depends upon its stability should have a gradient not exceeding 1 in 10 unless the truck or other vehicle has been specially designed or derated to suit any greater gradient.

2.1.5. Any permanent obstruction such as a lighting standard, crane track stanchion or other fixture likely to be a hazard to vehicles should be—

(*a*) clearly marked in alternating black and yellow stripes to a height of at least 2 m or as high as is practicable; and (*b*) fitted with local lighting unless the general lighting is sufficient to illuminate the stripes clearly.

2.2. Protection of edge

2.2.1. (1) Where a fork-lift truck or other vehicle is used regularly near the edge of a dock, that edge should be protected by a continuous coping wall or rigid barrier of sufficient strength to prevent the truck or other vehicle from accidentally falling into the water.

(2) Where possible, the wall or barrier should be sited on the inside of any bollard or capstan used for mooring a ship.

(3) Where the location recommended in subparagraph (2) is not practicable, gaps may be left in the wall or barrier, but such gaps should be no wider than is necessary to work the capstan, use the bollards or carry out any other operations required.

(4) In general, the wall or barrier should be as high as practicable, but not less than 30 cm in height.

2.2.2. Where a fork-lift truck or other vehicle is not used regularly near a dock edge, other suitable arrangements, such as a temporary barrier or positioning a second person to signal to the driver, should be made at any time when the truck or vehicle is operating dangerously near the edge.

2.3. Stacking goods or materials

2.3.1. Where goods or materials are stacked on a dock otherwise than in an intermodal freight container, the stacking should be carried out in an orderly and systematic manner. In particular—

(*a*) the method of stacking should comply with the requirements of Chapter 23;

(*b*) the stack should not be of such a height as to be unstable in high winds;

(*c*) where a dockworker is required to go on the top of a stack, safe means of access in accordance with the requirements of section 24.2 should be provided; and

(*d*) where goods or materials are stored at a dock edge, they should either—

(i) be placed in such a way that there is not enough room for a person to squeeze or attempt to squeeze between the stack and the dock edge; or

(ii) be deposited in such a way that there is a clear space of not less than 1.5 m between any part of the stack and the dock edge.

2.4. Fencing of dangerous edges

2.4.1. (1) Every break in a dock edge,[1] dangerous corner, walkway over a dock gate or caisson or similar dangerous place should, so far as is practicable, be fenced.

(2) The fencing should be—

(*a*) of sound material, good construction and adequate strength, free from any sharp edges and maintained in good order;

(*b*) at least 1 m high;

(*c*) consist of an upper and an intermediate rail or taut chain, the intermediate rail or chain being at a height of about 50 cm;

(*d*) have stanchions not more than 3 m apart; and

(*e*) in the case of an entrance to a dock gate or caisson, extend for a distance of at least 4.5 m on each side.

2.4.2. Chain should be used only where the fencing is of a collapsible or readily removable type to permit such operations as the mooring of ships and their passage through dock entrances.

---

[1] i.e. where steps lead down to the water's edge.

2.4.3. (1) Where chain is used, a means of keeping it taut should be provided.

(2) Where a portable stanchion fits into a socket or hole, it should be fitted to an adequate depth to maintain the stanchion as rigid as possible in the upright position, and the socket or hole should be kept clear of any substance or matter likely to prevent the stanchion from being completely inserted.

2.4.4. The fencing should be kept in position except to the extent to which its absence is necessary for the movement of a ship, the handling of goods or materials or the carrying out of repairs.

2.5. Rescue from drowning

2.5.1. Adequate and suitable life-saving equipment should be provided and maintained for the rescue of any person in danger of drowning.

(1) The rescue equipment should consist of lifebuoys, throwing buoys, grapnels, boathooks or any other suitable equipment.

(2) Throwing lines fitted to lifebuoys or similar equipment should be of suitable size and length, and should be made, whenever possible, of polypropylene in order that they will float.

(3) The equipment should be—

(*a*) located as near as practicable to the dock edge;

(*b*) kept free from obstruction, both physically and visually;

(*c*) regularly inspected by a responsible person; and

(*d*) hung or suitably contained in a case of adequate size and painted in a conspicuous colour.

2.5.2. A notice giving clear instructions for the resuscitation of a person rescued from drowning should be posted with the life-saving appliances.

2.5.3. (1) Ladders should be provided at every dock edge to

enable a person who has fallen into the water to climb to the top of the dockside. The ladders should be—

(*a*) spaced at intervals not exceeding 50 m;

(*b*) permanently positioned except at a part of a dock where it is not practicable to fit permanent ladders, and at which dockworkers do not have to be, or by which they do not have to pass, when there is no ship there; provided that temporary ladders shall be installed there while a ship is loading or unloading; and

(*c*) in conformity with the requirements of subparagraphs 3.6.1 (2) to (5) so far as is appropriate.

(2) Where it is not practicable for the ladder to extend at least 1 m above the top of the dock side, the stringers should extend as high as is practicable. Where no extension is practicable, adequate handholds should be provided in suitable recesses in the surface of the dock side.

(3) Where the stringers of the ladder extend beyond the top side, they should be opened out sufficiently in width (see subparagraph 3.7.1(3)(*d*)) to enable a person to pass through them, and they should be sloping or curved away from the dock edge.

(4) The bottom rung of the ladder should be at least 1 m below the lowest level of the water at any time.

(5) Unless a permanent ladder is recessed into the wall of the dock, it should be suitably protected on each side against damage from ships.

2.5.4. (1) Where work is proceeding aboard barges or similar vessels moored alongside a ship in a fast-flowing current, a suitable rowing or motor boat, according to the circumstances, should be provided where practicable and kept available for the rescue of any person who may fall into the water and be swept away.

(2) One or more suitable persons should be specially responsible for manning the boat in the event of an alarm.

2.6. Other dangers

2.6.1. (1) In areas of danger, a pedestrian route should be provided for persons requiring to make their way about the dock or any vessels that may be there. The route should be clearly marked.

(2) Where possible, the route should avoid any part regularly used by dock vehicles, such as the neighbourhood of stacks of goods and entrances to warehouses.

(3) Where the route has to cross an area used by vehicles, warning signs, permanent whenever possible, should be installed in a conspicuous position.

(4) Any corner where visibility is permanently obstructed by buildings or other structures should be provided with warning mirrors in order that pedestrians and drivers of vehicles can see each other approaching.

2.6.2. Where a temporary hole or trench is made in an area of essential use by vehicles and has to be temporarily bridged, the bridge should—

(*a*) be of adequate strength;

(*b*) have a sufficient overlap at the edge of the hole or trench;

(*c*) be of sufficient width;

(*d*) if used by pedestrians, be fenced on either side;

(*e*) bear a notice at each end stating that pedestrians should give way to vehicles;

(*f*) bear a notice at each end stating that vehicles should not attempt to pass on the bridge; and

(*g*) be provided with a ramp where there is an abrupt difference of levels.

3. Safe means of access

3.1. Means of access to ships

3.1.1. For the carrying out of dock work on board ship, sufficient safe and suitable means of access to the ship should be available for the use of dockworkers passing to and from the ship.

3.1.2. Whenever reasonably practicable, the means of access from the dock side should be the ship's accommodation ladder complying with the relevant requirements of section 3.2.

3.1.3. (1) Whenever the use of an accommodation ladder is not reasonably practicable, a gangway may be used.

(2) Rigid ladders may be used when gangways are not practicable.

(3) Gangways and ladders should comply with the relevant requirements of sections 3.3 and 3.4 respectively.

3.1.4. The means of access should be of sound material and construction and adequate strength, and be securely installed and kept in a good state of repair.

3.1.5. The means of access should be so placed that no loads pass over them.

3.1.6. Dockworkers should not use any means of access other than the means specified unless specially authorised to do so.

3.1.7. (1) The means of access from a ship to a barge or other vessel of low freeboard moored alongside it should be as stated in paragraph 3.1.3, except that a rope ladder may be used when it is impracticable to comply with the requirements of that paragraph.

(2) For the purposes of this code, "freeboard" means the height above water level of the deck used for access to the rope ladder when the access is used for the first time.

3.1.8. Where there is a gap between the dock side and the ship, such that a person falling from the ship's means of access would be in danger of falling into the water, that gap should be protected by a safety net secured to the ship and the dock side.

3.1.9. Any gap through which a person is liable to fall between the fencing of the means of access and the opening in the ship's bulwark should be properly protected.

3.1.10. The entrance should not be obstructed.

3.1.11. The means of access should not be placed so near to a crane track on the dock that it would be liable to be struck by a crane moving on that track.

3.1.12. Means of access manufactured of material other than wood or metal should be of equal strength and durability and of the same tread design.

3.1.13. When means of access are manufactured using components of dissimilar metals, suitable action should be taken to prevent wastage or corrosion due to galvanic action.

3.2. Ship's accommodation ladder

3.2.1. (1) A ship's accommodation ladder should have treads—

(*a*) at least 55 cm in width;

(*b*) of adequate depth;

(*c*) with a permanently non-slip surface; and

(*d*) of such a shape or design that at the working angle of the ladder a person's foot does not have to step upon a corner of the tread but upon a flat or curved surface.

(2) The accommodation ladder should be fenced on either side throughout its length with upper and intermediate guard rails of a height of not less than 1.1 m and 55 cm respectively, measured from the surface of the tread and at right angles to the longitudinal axis of the ladder.

(3) An adequate platform should be fitted at either end of the ladder as necessary.

(4) The construction of the ladder should be sufficiently robust to reduce any sway or bounce to a minimum.

(5) The ladder should be properly rigged and be kept adjusted in such a way that—

(*a*) whatever the state of the tide or the draught of the ship, the ladder's angle to the horizontal does not exceed approximately 40° so far as is practicable; and

(*b*) it is safe to pass from the lowest tread or the platform of the ladder on to the dock.

(6) As far as is practicable, the ladder should be kept free of any snow, ice, grease or other substance likely to render handhold or foothold insecure.

(7) Existing accommodation ladders with fixed flat treads should, when situated at such an angle as to require persons to walk on the edge of the treads, be fitted with properly secured covering boards with transverse treads located at suitable intervals (cleated duck boards).

3.3. Gangways

3.3.1. A gangway should—

(*a*) have a closely boarded walkway at least 55 cm in width;

(*b*) be fitted with transverse treads at suitable stepping intervals;

(*c*) be fitted with upper and intermediate guard rails complying with the requirements of subparagraph 3.2.1(2); and

(*d*) be fitted with devices enabling it to be properly secured to the ship.

3.3.2. If its weight is such that a lifting appliance has to be used to place it in position, the gangway should be fitted with proper slinging attachments so placed that it will balance about the attachments when it is suspended.

3.3.3. A gangway should be installed to comply with the requirements of subparagraph 3.2.1(5)(*a*).

3.3.4. Where a gangway rests upon a ship's bulwark, safe means of access should be provided for a person to pass to and from the ship's deck to the walkway of the gangway.

3.3.5. Where a gangway rests on the dock upon a roller or wheels, they should be either so fitted or so guarded as to prevent a person's foot from being caught between the roller or a wheel and the dock surface.

3.3.6. The gangway should be so positioned that the roller or each wheel is on a reasonably level surface and not in the vicinity of any obstruction or hole that would be apt to restrict free movement of the roller or wheel.

3.3.7. Any gap between the end of a gangway and the adjacent ship's rails through which a person is liable to fall should be properly protected.

3.4. Portable ladders

3.4.1. Every portable ladder used by a dockworker should be of sound material, of good construction, of adequate strength and properly maintained.

3.4.2. Every portable ladder other than a rope ladder should—

(*a*) have rungs equally spaced apart at intervals of not less than 25 cm or more than 35 cm;

(*b*) have rungs of a width between its uprights of not less than 38 cm or more than 45 cm; and

(*c*) not as a general rule exceed 6 m in a single length.

3.4.3. A wooden ladder should—

(*a*) have uprights made of suitable wood with the grain running lengthwise;

(*b*) have rungs properly secured to the uprights; nails or spikes should not be used for this purpose;

(*c*) not be painted, but treated with clear varnish or other effective preservative of a type that would not conceal any defect that would otherwise be visible; and (*d*) where necessary, be provided with a sufficient number of metal cross-ties.

3.4.4. A ladder constructed of lightweight metal should have—

(*a*) uprights that are—

(i) made in one continuous length and of sufficiently large cross-section to prevent dangerous deflection of the ladder when in use; and

(ii) fitted with non-slip shoes or other suitable means of reducing the ladder's slippage to a minimum; and

(*b*) rungs that are—

(i) of adequate diameter (in any event not less than 20 mm) secured to the uprights in such a way that they are not apt to work loose, and in particular to turn; and

(ii) corrugated to minimise the danger of slippage of a person's foot.

3.4.5. A straight extension ladder should—

(*a*) when extended, not exceed 15 m in length;

(*b*) be equipped with suitable guide brackets and an effective locking device so that each extension is securely held and locked in the desired position;

(*c*) be extended by ropes that should be securely anchored and run over pulleys having a groove suited to the rope size; and

(*d*) not have more than two extending sections.

3.4.6. (1) When a ladder other than a rope ladder is in use—

(*a*) the top should rise at least 1 m above the landing place or the highest point to be reached by a person using the ladder; and

(*b*) the ladder should not stand upon any loose packing but each upright should properly rest upon a firm and level footing.

(2) A ladder other than a rope ladder should be prevented from displacement or slipping—

(*a*) by being securely fixed at its upper resting position; or (*b*) if it cannot be secured at the top, by being securely fixed at its base; or

(*c*) if fastening at the base is also impracticable, by having a person stationed at the foot.

(3) A straight ladder over 6 m in length should where practicable be additionally secured at a point situated one-third of the way along the ladder, measured from the bottom.

3.4.7. Each ladder should be inspected at suitable intervals by a responsible person, and if dangerous defects are found the ladder should be immediately taken out of service.

3.4.8. Workers using a ladder should—

(*a*) have both hands free for climbing up and down;

(*b*) face the ladder when climbing up and down;

(*c*) avoid wearing footwear that is slippery;

(*d*) avoid carrying heavy or bulky loads; and

(*e*) use belts or other suitable means to carry any object they may need.

3.4.9. A portable metal ladder should not be used in any place where any part of it is apt to come into contact with an overhead power cable, traveller conductor wires or any other electrical equipment comprising bare live metal parts until the danger has been eliminated by switching off and isolating the power.

3.5. Rope ladders

3.5.1. A rope ladder should not be used for any purpose other than providing access from a ship to a barge or similar vessel of lower freeboard.

3.5.2. Every rope ladder should comply with the requirements of paragraph 3.4.1.

3.5.3. A rope ladder should be fitted with treads that—

(*a*) are made of ash, oak, elm or teak, or other suitable material, unpainted and free from knots, except that the four lowest treads may be made of rubber of sufficient strength and stiffness and of the same shape and dimensions as the wooden treads;

(*b*) provide a foothold of not less than 11.5 cm in depth and not less than 40 cm in width;

(*c*) have a non-slip top surface so far as is practicable; and

(*d*) are secured at each end to two supporting ropes in such a manner that the treads are firmly held against any twist, turnover or tilt.

3.5.4. (1) The rope ladder should be fitted with spreaders at intervals not greater than nine treads apart.

(2) Each spreader should—

(*a*) be made in one piece;

(*b*) have an over-all length of not less than 1.8 m; and

(*c*) be secured to the back of a tread by means of countersunk brass screws in such a way that it extends for an equal length on either side of the ladder.

3.5.5. The rope ladder should be so rigged that—

(*a*) its two suspension ropes on either side are, so far as is reasonably practicable, in equal tension, properly secured to the ship; and

(*b*) the treads are horizontal.

3.5.6. Safe access should be provided between—

(*a*) the top of the ladder and the deck of the ship; and

(*b*) the barge or other vessel and the lower part of the ladder.

3.5.7. Where practicable, the ladder should hang fully extended when in use and should not be positioned over or in close proximity to a discharge opening in the ship's side.

3.6. Access to ship's hold

3.6.1. (1) Where practicable, the access of persons to a ship's hold should be by means of a separate man-hatch and a permanent ladder separate from the hold. Where possible the ladder should be sloping.

(2) A sloping ladder may be fitted with single rungs, provided that its angle to the vertical does not exceed 15°. Otherwise it should be fitted either with treads or with pairs of rungs.

(3) The treads or rungs should—

(*a*) be equally spaced at intervals of 30 cm apart;

(*b*) provide a foothold of not less than 11.5 cm in depth and not less than 35 cm in width;

(*c*) in the case of double rungs, be fitted adjacent to each other on the same horizontal level with the clear gap between them not exceeding 5 cm;

(*d*) in the case of rungs made from solid bar steel, have a diameter of not less than 25 mm, and in the case of rungs made from square bar steel, the sides of the square should not be less than 22 mm; and

(*e*) be horizontal.

(4) The ladder should have the following clearances:

(*a*) behind the tread or rung (in the case of double rungs, the rear rung), not less than 15 cm for the user's foot;

(*b*) in front, for the user's body, not less than 76 cm in the case of a vertical ladder and 1 m in the case of a sloping ladder (measured at right angles to the axis of the ladder); and

(*c*) at the side, not less than 75 mm for the user's hand.

(5) In general, a ladder should—

(*a*) if its own length, or if the total length of ladders that lie in the same line, exceeds 6 m, be provided with suitable landing platforms for every 6 m of length or fraction thereof;

(*b*) have landings of a suitable size and protected on each side, other than the side on which the ladder is fitted, with a rigid guard rail fitted at a height of about 1 m above the platform;

(*c*) have uprights that are smoothly finished;

(*d*) have treads that should either be of chequer plate or have another equally effective non-slip surface;

(*e*) have treads with a front edge that is radiused;

(*f*) if welded, have welds with a generous fillet—reliance should not be made on butt welding alone; and

(*g*) be secured to the bulkhead at intervals not exceeding 2.5 m apart to prevent vibration.

(6) A separate man-hatch giving access to a ladder should—

(*a*) have a clear opening not less than 60 cm by 60 cm;

(*b*) be fitted with a coaming not less than 15 cm high;

(*c*) be provided with adequate handhold fitted clear of the coaming; and

(*d*) have its hatch cover, if any, provided with adequate securing arrangements, particularly where the handhold required by (*c*) is fitted to the inside of the cover.

3.6.2. (1) Where it is not possible to provide the access required by subparagraph 3.6.1(1), access to the hold should, whenever possible, be by—

(*a*) a ladder or ladders complying with the requirements of subparagraph 3.6.1(2) to 3.6.1(5); and

(*b*) steps, cleats or cups.

(2) The ladder should extend to the underside of the hatch covers when this is practicable.

(3) A ladder should not be recessed without a platform.

(4) Whenever possible, a ladder should be provided at each end of the hatch.

(5) Where it is not practicable for the ladder to extend to the

underside of the hatch cover, steps, cleats or cups should be fitted in line with the ladder. The steps, cleats or cups should—

(*a*) provide a foothold of not less than 15 cm in depth and 30 cm in width;

(*b*) provide a firm handhold and be so constructed as to prevent the foot from slipping sideways off the step or cleat;

(*c*) be continued to within at least 45 cm of the top of the coaming; and

(*d*) comply with the requirements of paragraph 3.6.1.

(6) Where the top of the coaming is of such a width that a person using the means of access provided under paragraph 3.6.2 cannot obtain a safe grasp, a suitable handhold should be provided at or near the coaming top on both inner and outer sides.

(7) Coamings that have a height greater than 1 m above the deck should be provided with steps or cleats complying with the requirements of subparagraph 3.6.2(5) or other suitable access.

(8) The access to the coaming where the ladders, steps, cleats or cups are fitted shall be kept free from obstruction of any substance likely to make footholds insecure.

(9) Where permanent ship's fittings such as pipes pass along the deck at the base or side of the coamings, suitable access over these should be provided. Where a permanent platform is fitted for this purpose, the distance from the top of the platform to the top of the coaming should not be less than 76 cm.

(10) Where a hold ladder leads to the top of a deep tank or a shaft tunnel—

(*a*) a ladder, cleat or steps complying with the preceding provisions of this paragraph should be provided to enable a person to pass to and from the tank or the shaft tunnel to the bottom of the hold; and

(*b*) an adequate handhold should be provided at the top of the tank or the shaft tunnel.

(11) Where it is possible to stow cargo at the back of a hold ladder, a clearance of not less than 15 cm should be left between the cargo and any tread or rung of the ladder.

(12) Where the ladder, steps, cleats or cups in a ship's hold are obstructed by cargo and it is necessary to use a portable ladder to gain access, that ladder should comply, so far as is appropriate, with the requirements of section 3.4.

(13) In the case of barge or inland vessel of similar low draught having a hold or holds not exceeding 3.5 m in depth and on which the fitting of permanent means of access into the hold is not reasonably practicable, either a portable ladder complying with the requirements of section 3.4 or preferably a steel detachable ladder should be used.

(14) A steel detachable ladder should comply with the requirements of paragraph 3.6.2 so far as is appropriate, except that if its uprights are of tubular construction the tube should have a diameter of not less than 30 mm and a wall thickness of not less than 2.5 mm, and if its rungs are made of square bar steel the side of the square should not be less than 16 mm. The attachment arrangements should be such that the ladder is securely held in position and will not be accidentally displaced when in use. Each ladder should be fitted in a position where it is not liable to be damaged by swinging cargo.

3.7. Access to lifting appliances

3.7.1. (1) Safe means of access shall be provided to the cabin and any other part of a lifting appliance to which a dockworker is required to go in the course of his work.

(2) A ladder used for this purpose should—

(*a*) be of steel construction and comply with the relevant requirements of section 3.6; and

(*b*) where practicable, be sloping and be installed inside the superstructure of the appliance.

(3) The stringers of the ladder should—

(*a*) where possible, be in one continuous length; provided that where a join is necessary and a fish plate is used, the plate should be fitted on the inside of the stringers;

(*b*) be adequately supported from the structure at suitable intervals;

(*c*) extend at least 1 m above the landing platform; and

(*d*) where the ladder gives access to a platform from the outside of the platform, be opened out above platform level to give a clear width of 70 to 75 cm to enable a person to pass through the stringers.

(4) Where the slope of a ladder exceeds 15° to the vertical, the ladder should be provided with suitable handrails not less than 54 cm apart, measured horizontally.

(5) The vertical height of the ladder should not in general exceed 3 m.

(6) A ladder should not slope more than 25° to the vertical.

(7) Where the slope exceeds 15° to the vertical, the front of any tread should overlap the next lowest tread by at least 16 mm.

3.7.2. A vertical ladder of a height exceeding 3 m and any ladder less than 3 m high that is so placed as to expose a dockworker to falling into a hold should be fitted with guard hoops which should—

(*a*) be uniformly spaced at intervals not exceeding 90 cm apart;

(*b*) have a clearance of 75 cm from the rung to the back of the hoop; and

(*c*) be connected by longitudinal strips secured to the inside of the hoops, each equally spaced round the circumference of the hoop.

3.7.3. (1) Where a ladder gives access to the outside of the platform, the stringers should be connected at their extremities to the guard rails of the platform, irrespective of whether the ladder is sloping or vertical.

(2) In the case of a vertical ladder, the final hoop should be fitted to the extremities of the stringers.

3.7.4. Where a ladder gives access to a platform through a hole in the platform, either—

(*a*) an adequate handhold should be provided on the platform; or, preferably—

(*b*) (i) the stringers should be carried above the floor level of the platform to at least 1 m; and

(ii) the extremities of the stringers should be given lateral support and the top step or rung should be level with the floor of the platform unless the steps or rungs are fitted to the extremities of the stringers.

3.7.5. Where a platform is provided it should—

(*a*) have a minimum dimension of at least 75 cm in either direction;

(*b*) be fitted with a guard rail and an intermediate rail, the guard rail being not less than 1 m above the floor of the platform;

(*c*) be fitted with a toe board extending to a height of not less than 15 cm above the floor of the platform;

(*d*) have a floor of non-slip construction; and

(*e*) have a minimum headroom under any obstacle of not less than 2.1 m.

3.7.6. Where a ladder unavoidably leads on to a platform at a position where a slewing or moving part of the lifting appliance is apt to strike or trap a person ascending on to the platform—

(*a*) a person should not ascend until clearance has been received from the driver of the appliance that it is safe to ascend;

(*b*) the entrance to the platform should be fitted with a self-closing door of suitable construction which, in the case of a hinged door, should swing inwards on to the platform; and

(*c*) the door should be fitted with a permanently legible warning notice.

3.7.7. All ladders and platforms should be adequately illuminated at all times when the appliance is in use.

3.8. Transport of persons by water

3.8.1. (1) When dockworkers have to be transported to or from a ship or any other place, suitable and proper measures should be taken to provide for their safe passage.

(2) In particular, the boat used should be—

(*a*) of suitable construction, properly equipped for use and navigation and maintained in a seaworthy state; and

(*b*) manned by an adequate and experienced crew under the charge of a competent person.

3.8.2. In the case of a boat driven by mechanical power—

(*a*) the number of persons the boat can safely carry should be certified by a competent person and displayed on the boat in a conspicuous place;

(*b*) sufficient seating accommodation should be provided for all persons carried, at least 50 per cent of it being under cover and the remainder being protected from the weather so far as is practicable;

(*c*) an adequate supply of suitable fire extinguishers should be carried; and

(*d*) to protect a person from falling overboard, the boat should have either a bulwark at least 60 cm or rigid rail at least 75 cm high.

3.8.3. (1) Embarkation and disembarkation should take place only at suitable and safe landing places.

(2) The landing place shall be provided with suitable bollards, cleats or other arrangements of adequate strength to which the boat may be made fast.

(3) A bridge or gangway leading on to a pontoon should comply with the requirements of section 3.3.

(4) Permanent steps leading down to a pontoon or landing place from a dock side should be provided with a permanent fixed handrail on the wall side and with chain fencing complying with the require-

ments of paragraphs 2.4.1 to 2.4.3 on the waterside. The chain should be unhooked only to the extent necessary for boarding or leaving the boat and should be replaced when the steps are not in use.

(5) Every landing place should be provided with an adequate supply of suitable life-saving equipment maintained in a fit state for ready use together.

(6) The pontoon or landing place should be provided with hanging chains extending into the water for the support of the persons who have fallen in.

(7) There should be posted in a conspicuous position a notice giving clear instructions for the resuscitation of a person rescued from drowning.

(8) Pontoons, landing places, bridges, gangways and steps should be adequately lighted.

3.8.4. All dockworkers should—

(*a*) obey any instructions relating to their safety or the safety of the boat in which they are travelling given by the competent person in charge of the boat; and

(*b*) embark and disembark only when the boat is properly moored and then do so in an orderly fashion.

3.9. Protection of hatches

3.9.1. Every cargo hatchway should be protected by means of a coaming or fencing to a height of at least 1 m above the deck or any other level at which a dockworker may be expected to stand.

3.9.2. (1) The cargo hatchway fencing should consist of rigid rails.

(2) Suitable wire rope or chain may be used for fencing, provided that—

(*a*) means are fitted for keeping the wire rope or chain as taut as is practicable;

(*b*) where wire rope is used for fencing, it has sufficient wires per strand to make it flexible;

(*c*) wire ropes are free from broken wires; and

(*d*) any loose ends of wire ropes are fitted with compressed metal ferrules or other suitable means of protection to prevent injury to a person.

(3) Sufficient stanchions should be provided.

(4) When the stanchions fit into sockets in the deck, the sockets should be so designed as to prevent the stanchions from moving unduly out of their vertical position or from being accidentally displaced; in particular, each socket should be sufficiently deep and equipped with a locking device.

(5) The fencing itself and the fittings for securing it should be provided by the ship's owner and should form a permanent part of the ship's equipment.

(6) The fencing required under paragraph 3.9.1 should be kept in place at all times, except—

(*a*) when the cargo hatch is being opened or closed; or

(*b*) when goods are being loaded on to the particular deck and the general unloading or loading of the hold prevents the cargo hatch from being closed; or

(*c*) during a meal break or other similar short interruption of work.

3.9.3. (1) No fork-lift truck or other vehicle should be used on any 'tween deck unless either the hatch cover is strong enough for the truck or vehicle in its loaded state or a suitable overlay is provided.

(2) The maximum concentrated load (in tonnes) that may be applied to a hatch cover shall be conspicuously marked on or near the hatch cover.

(3) A fork-lift truck or other vehicle should not be allowed on to a hatch having wooden covers unless an overlay of adequate strength is placed upon the covers.

3.10. Hatch beams and hatch covers

3.10.1. Hatch covers and hatch beams, together with hatch beam locking devices, should be of good construction and maintained in a good condition.

3.10.2. Broken, split, poorly fitting or otherwise defective covers and beams should not be used and should be immediately repaired or replaced.

3.10.3. Wooden covers should be bound with steel bands or straps. The bands or straps should be kept firmly secured in place, particularly at their ends.

3.10.4. (1) Where a hatch cover is required to be lifted by hand, it should be fitted with suitable hand grips of sufficient size to enable a hand to obtain a proper grasp, and for the hand to be immediately released and withdrawn in the event of the cover's accidentally falling.

(2) Wherever practicable, hand grips should be fitted diagonally.

(3) Hand grips should be inspected before each occasion of use, and if any are found to be missing or defective the necessary replacements or repairs should be made immediately by the ship's officers.

3.10.5. Hatch covers and beams should be plainly marked to indicate the hatch, deck and section to which they belong unless all the hatch covers and beams are interchangeable or, in respect of marking of position, where all parts of a hatch cover are interchangeable.

3.10.6. Every hatch beam, pontoon or similar cover should be of such length that when the beam or cover is moved horizontally in the direction of its length as far as it will go in one direction, the other end still rests upon its support, overlapping its end support surfaces by at least 65 mm in the case of covers and 75 mm in the case of beams.

3.10.7. (1) Every hatch beam or pontoon should be fitted with an effective locking device such that when it is locked in position it cannot become accidentally displaced.

(2) The device should be strong enough to withstand without damage a reasonable blow from any swinging cargo.

3.10.8. (1) If the hatch is fitted with rolling or sliding beams—

(*a*) the top guide should project over the roller or end of the beam, as the case may be, in such a way that when a beam is moved horizontally in the direction of its length as far as it will go in one direction, the other end is still retained by its top guide; and

(*b*) lateral movement of a rolling or sliding beam in the horizontal direction of its length should be restricted in such a way that in the event of its crabbing it will seize before an end can slip off its guide.

(2) When a rolling or sliding beam seizes in position whilst being moved, no attempt should be made to release it by bumping it with a suspended load or by hauling on it by means of a wire rope reeved on the warping drum of a winch. The matter should be reported to a ship's officer.

3.10.9 (1) Every hatch beam and cover that has to be removed by the use of a lifting appliance should be fitted with suitable attachments for securing the lifting slings.

(2) In the case of a beam, the attachments should be so positioned that it is not necessary for a person to go upon it to secure the sling or slings.

(3) For lifting pontoons four-legged slings should be used.

(4) Slings should be long enough to reach easily the holes at the ends of the beam when forming an angle not exceeding 120°.

(5) Each leg of all beam and pontoon slings should be equipped with a substantial lanyard at least 3 m long.

3.10.10. (1) It should be the duty of the employer of the dock-workers to replace the fencing on cessation of work for any extensive period (i.e. a period other than a temporary break such as a meal break).

(2) The requirement in subparagraph (1) may be waived if the

employer has previously given written notice to the officer in charge of the ship, on a specially printed form, that the hatchway is open and has been left unfenced, and if that notice has been acknowledged in writing by the officer.

(3) It should be the responsibility of the officer in charge upon receipt and acknowledgement of the notice either to fence or close the hatch or to take any other effective steps to ensure that no dockworker can fall into the unprotected hatch opening.

3.10.11. (1) Hatch covers and beams should be plainly marked to indicate the hatch, deck and section to which they belong.

(2) The requirement in subparagraph (1) may be waived in respect of hatch and deck markings in cases in which all the hatch covers of a ship are interchangeable and, in respect of section markings, in cases in which all parts of a hatch cover are interchangeable.

3.11. Mechanically, hydraulically and electrically powered hatch covers

3.11.1. Mechanically, hydraulically and electrically powered hatch covers should be opened and closed only by designated members of the ship's crew or by other authorised persons.

3.11.2 No dockworker should be required to be in a position of danger during the actual opening and closing of the hatch.

3.11.3 (1) No person should be permitted on any hatch cover, whether closed or retracted, when it is about to be opened or closed as the case may be.

(2) Folding hatch covers should be fitted with locking devices, wheel chocks or other suitable means to prevent the covers from spontaneously folding back when they are released from their coaming seals.

(3) No person should be permitted on the top of retracted backfolding hatch covers unless the preventer chains or other securing devices are in position.

(4) If a hatchway is fitted with a hatch covered by this section, loading or unloading should not take place at that hatch unless the covers are secured in the open position or are of such design as to render inadvertent abrupt closing impossible.

3.11.4. Persons should be warned, by warning devices or otherwise, when hatch covers are about to be opened or closed.

3.12. Cargo gangways

3.12.1. Cargo gangways should be made of sound material, substantially and firmly constructed, adequately supported, if necessary securely fastened, and maintained in good repair.

3.12.2. Cargo gangways should not be overloaded.

3.12.3. Cargo gangways other than chutes should be at least 1 m wide, and if at any point their height exceeds 1.5 m from quay or ship they should be provided with railings complying with the relevant requirements of section 2.4.

3.12.4. Cargo gangways should not be so steep as to cause danger or undue fatigue.

3.12.5. (1) On sloping gangways, transverse treads should be fitted at suitable stepping intervals.

(2) If trucks are used, the treads should be suitably shortened.

3.13. Portable lighting

3.13.1. (1) It should be prohibited to enter unlighted or inadequately lighted places on the ship without safe enclosed portable lights.

(2) Such lights should be readily available.

3.13.2. The use of open lights in holds should be prohibited.

3.13.3. Portable lights should be equipped with adequate guards to prevent flammable and other combustible material from coming into contact with them.

3.13.4. Lighting for use in holds where there is an explosion risk should be of a suitable flameproof type for the atmosphere in question.

3.14. Escape facilities

3.14.1. Precautions should be taken to facilitate the escape of dockworkers when handling coal or other bulk cargo in a hold or on 'tween decks.

3.15. Handling of covers and beams

3.15.1. Hatchways should be opened sufficiently to allow loads to be safely hoisted or lowered.

3.15.2. Before work is begun at a hatch, the beams should either be removed or be securely fastened to prevent their displacement.

3.15.3. Hatch covers that cannot easily be handled by two workers should not be handled manually.

3.15.4. Dockworkers removing and replacing hatch covers by hand should—

(*a*) work from the centre towards the sides when removing covers and from the sides towards the centre when replacing covers; and

(*b*) use suitable long-handled hooks so as to avoid stooping when grasping the covers.

3.15.5. Dockworkers pulling tarpaulins should where possible walk forwards, not backwards, when working on hatch covers.

3.15.6. When being replaced, hatch covers and pontoons and beams should be placed on the hatches in the position indicated by the markings, and should be adequately secured.

3.15.7. Hatch covers and pontoons and beams should not be removed or replaced while work is going on in the hold under the hatchway.

3.15.8. Hatch covers and pontoons should not be used in the construction of cargo stages or for any other purpose that might expose them to damage.

3.15.9. Hatch covers, pontoons, tarpaulins, fore-and-aft beams and thwartship beams which have been removed should be so laid down, stacked or secured that they cannot fall into the hold or otherwise cause danger.

3.15.10. Hatch covers and pontoons should either be arranged in neat piles not higher than the coaming and away from it, or be spread one high between coaming and rail with no space between them.[1]

3.15.11. (1) Beams should either be laid on their sides or be stood on edge close together; they should be lashed to prevent the outside ones from being overturned, and they should be wedged if that is necessary to prevent tilting.

(2) If beams are convex underneath, they should be wedged at each end.

(3) The height of stacks should be regulated so that if accidentally struck by a sling they will not endanger men working below or overside.

3.15.12. Hatch covers, pontoons and beams should be so placed as to leave a safe walkway from rail to hatch coaming or fore and aft.

3.15.13. A space of at least 1 m should be left between hatch covers, pontoons and beams that have been removed and the hatchway, if the construction of the ship so allows.

3.16. Work in holds

3.16.1. (1) Cargo should be so stowed in 'tween decks with due regard to the order of unloading that when 'tween-deck hatch covers and beams have to be removed there will be a working space 1 m wide between the stowed cargo and the coaming.

---

[1] It is recommended that on the working side of the hatch the top level of the pontoons or hatch covers be 15 cm or more below the top edge of the coaming.

(2) No such space need be left free on the covered portion of a partly opened hatch, but measures should be taken to prevent stowed cargo from falling into the open section.

3.16.2. The stowing, handling and stacking or unstacking of goods should be done under competent supervision.

3.16.3. When cargo is built up in sections in the hold, each section should allow for a safe landing place for cargo.

3.16.4. If there is a risk that dockworkers may fall from a height of more than 2 m during the work, suitable measures should be taken where practicable by installing fences, guard rails or nets.

3.16.5. No more gangs of dockworkers should be put to work in a hold than is permissible for safe working.

3.16.6. Where two or more gangs are working in the same hatch—

(*a*) there should be a separate signaller for each fall worked, except in the case of union purchase; and
(*b*) where gangs are working at different levels, a net should be rigged and securely fastened to prevent dockworkers from falling down or cargo from falling on to dockworkers below.

3.16.7. When cargo is worked in the ship's hold, there should be a safe place and safe passage for the signaller on the deck cargo or on the deck.

3.16.8. No loose gear or other objects should be thrown into or out of holds.

3.16.9. During the loading of bulk cargo, care should be taken to check trimmers in and out.

3.16.10. When bulk cargo is being unloaded, the worker attending the plant in the hold should if necessary be secured by a safety belt and life line.

3.16.11. Explosives and other dangerous cargo should be handled in conformity with the relevant requirements of section 26.1.

3.16.12. Stowing winches should be properly secured to prevent shifting.

4. Lifting appliances and other cargo-handling appliances[1]

4.1. Definitions

4.1.1. For the purposes of sections 4.11 to 4.13—

(*a*) a "limit switch" (4.11) is a device that automatically limits the extent of the movement of a crane or any part of a crane by cutting off the power at the limits;

(*b*) an "automatic overload cut-out" (4.12) is a device that automatically limits the load on a crane or part of a crane by cutting off the power when that load exceeds the safe working load;

(*c*) an "indicator of safe working load" (4.13) is a device that automatically indicates visually (whether a load is suspended or not) the crane designer's safe working load rating of the crane at the various radii of the load.

4.2. General provisions

4.2.1. Every lifting appliance and other cargo-handling appliance should—

(*a*) be of good design and construction, and of adequate strength for the purpose for which it is used;

(*b*) conform to the national or international standards that apply;

(*c*) be maintained in good repair and working order;

(*d*) be properly installed and used;

(*e*) before being taken into use for the first time, or after any substantial alteration or repair and periodically thereafter, be tested, thoroughly examined and certificated by a competent person in

---

[1] Other than mobile cranes, for which see Chapter 5.

accordance with the requirements of Appendices A, C and D; and

(*f*) be operated only by thoroughly trained drivers who have passed tests for ability to operate the appliance safely.

4.2.2. (1) A cargo gear register and related certificates concerning machinery and gear of such types as to require initial and/or periodic testing and/or examinations and inspection should be kept and be available.

(2) The content and layout of the documents should be as established by the competent authority and in accordance with the model documents recommended by the International Labour Office.

(3) In the case of shore-located cranes and similar equipment, the competent authority may adopt different documents, provided that the necessary information is clearly provided.

4.2.3. Registers and certificates for gear currently aboard ship or ashore should be preserved for at least four years after the date of last entry.

4.3. Controls

4.3.1. (1) Any controls should be so located that the driver at his stand or seat has ample room for operation.

(2) In particular, there should be the following clearances above the head of the operator:

(*a*) in the case of a seated operator, not less than 1 m measured to the point of maximum depression of the seat; and

(*b*) in the case of a standing operator, not less than 2 m from the platform on which he stands.

(3) The movement of controls to produce the desired action should—

(*a*) in the case of a hand lever, not exceed 60 cm at the handle of the lever;

(*b*) in the case of a foot pedal, not exceed 25 cm.

(4) Every foot control should have a non-slip surface.

4.3.2. Controls should be—

(*a*) positioned with due regard to ergonometric considerations;

(*b*) so positioned that the operator has an unrestricted view of the particular operation or of any person who may be authorised to give him signals for the operation;

(*c*) marked with their purpose and method of operation, which should be in accordance with the following provisions:

 (i) when a vertical lever is pulled towards the operator, a horizontal lever is raised or a swivelling lever or handwheel is moved clockwise, the load, and in the case of a derricking jib control the jib, should rise or the appliance should move backwards;

 (ii) when a vertical lever is pushed away from the operator, a horizontal lever is lowered or a swivelling lever or handwheel is moved anti-clockwise, the load, and in the case of a derricking jib control the jib, should descend or the appliance should move forward; and

 (iii) in the case of an appliance or part of an appliance having a slewing motion, the appliance or its part should slew clockwise when its control device is turned clockwise or moved to the right, and vice versa.

4.3.3. The operating pedals of a fork-lift truck or other dock transport vehicle should be so positioned that—

(*a*) the clutch (when fitted) is on the left of the operator's feet;

(*b*) the accelerator or other power control is on the right of the operator's feet; and

(*c*) the brake is between the two other pedals.

4.3.4. Effective means of keeping controls in the neutral position should be provided for all controls that have such a position.

4.3.5. If controls include a long horizontal lever, it should be fitted with a counterbalance weight, and if the weight is movable there should be provided an effective means of locking it in any position.

4.3.6. On "dead man's" controls fitted with a spring or other suitable means to return the controls to the "stop" position when the operator's hand is released or relaxed, the device should not be so strong as to cause operator fatigue.

4.3.7. Control handles on a power truck or tractor should be protected by design or by guards against accidental contact with fixed or moving objects that might cause an unexpected movement of the vehicle or result in injuries to the driver's hands or fingers.

4.3.8. Electrically driven winches and cranes should be so installed that—

(*a*) the hoisting motor can be started only when the controls have passed through neutral;

(*b*) when auxiliary current is supplied, a short circuit in the auxiliary current system cannot lead the hoisting motor to start or continue to run, or the brake to be released or remain released.

4.3.9. A suitably located auxiliary switch by means of which the current can be switched off should be provided immediately adjacent to the place where electrically driven winches are operated.

4.3.10. Winches and cranes driven by internal combustion engines should be so constructed that the load cannot fall by its own weight when the hoisting engine is disconnected.

4.4. Brakes

4.4.1. Every motor should be fitted with a brake which—

(*a*) if hand-operated, should not require a force greater than 160N (16 kgf); and (*b*) if foot-operated, should not require a force greater than 320N (32 kgf).

4.4.2. (1) An automatically applied brake should operate—

(*a*) when the control lever is returned to its neutral position;

(*b*) when any emergency stop is operated; and

(*c*) where there is any failure in the power supply, including complete failure of a phase or a significant drop in voltage.

(2) The design should be such that the operating solenoid cannot be accidentally energised by the back electromotive force of any motor driven by the crane, by a stray or rogue current or by breakdown of any insulation.

4.4.3. Whether applied by hand, by the foot or automatically, a brake should be able to exert a braking torque 25 per cent in excess of the torque required when the maximum safe working load is being carried under the most adverse working conditions, irrespective of losses in the transmission machinery.

4.4.4. (1) A slewing brake should be capable of holding the jib stationary when it is at its maximum radius with the maximum safe working load suspended from it and with the wind loading acting on the crane with a force not greater than that for which the crane has been designed.

(2) In the case of a lifting appliance installed on board a ship and designed to operate with the ship having a specified amount of list or trim, the brake specifications should allow for the additional force required to overcome the effects of the deviation from the vertical.

4.4.5. The brake fitted to any slewing part of a crane should be combined with a slipping clutch or other device to prevent the slewing motion from being stopped too suddenly.

4.4.6. In the case of a crane designed in such a manner as to allow the load to descend under the influence of gravity, an automatically applied speed limiting brake should be fitted in addition to the normal brake to ensure that the load cannot descend at a dangerous speed.

4.4.7. (1) The contact surface of a brake should be machined to a smooth surface finish and be free from any defect.

(2) The brake lining or pads in the case of disc brakes should be properly secured.

(3) The design should be such that the brake lining or pads remain adequately secured during their working life.

4.4.8. Unless the brake is self-adjusting, appropriate means should be provided to permit brake adjustment to be carried out readily and without danger to any person.

4.4.9. No adjustment of any brake should be carried out unless any torque acting on the brake drum or disc has been removed.

4.4.10. The brake drum should be protected from the ingress of any rain, sea water, snow, ice, oil or grease unless the brake has been designed, as, for example, on a simple ship's winch, to operate satisfactorily without such protection.

4.5. Lubrication

4.5.1. Every greasing and lubrication point should be so placed that grease or oil can be applied without danger to the person.

4.5.2. (1) As a general rule, it should not be necessary to remove any guard protecting dangerous machinery.

(2) Where it is necessary to remove the guard, the lubrication should be done by remote means, from outside the space that is normally guarded.

4.6. Rope lead

4.6.1. (1) A wire rope should be properly led on to its winding drum, and the angle of lead should be sufficiently small to ensure that the rope does not receive accumulative damage, particularly where it climbs from one layer to the next. (As a general rule the angle between the rope and a plane perpendicular to the axis of the drum should not exceed 1 in 16 for hoisting ropes and 1 in 12 for derricking ropes.)

(2) Where it would not be possible otherwise to avoid an excessive angle of lead, a suitable coiling or spooling device should be fitted.

4.7. Rope drums

4.7.1. The rope drum should be of the largest practicable diameter.

4.7.2. (1) The rope drum should be fitted with flanges of adequate diameter, particularly in the case of a cargo winch drum where it is not practicable to reel the rope on in orderly layers.

(2) Where the drum has a gear wheel at one end, this may be accepted as a flange, provided there is a plain part projecting at least 2.5 rope diameters beyond the outer layer of the rope when the latter is fully wound on the drum.

4.7.3. (1) If the drum is grooved, the whole of the working length of the rope should be accommodated in not more than three complete layers.

(2) If the drum is not grooved, the winding surface should, if possible, be of an area sufficient to accommodate the whole of the working length of the rope in one layer.

4.7.4. In the case of a winch serving a ship's crane, ship's derrick or derrick crane, the derricking and hoisting drums should be capable of accommodating a working length of rope sufficient for lifting a load from the ship's tank top with the jib or boom at its highest working position and from the floor of a lighter's hold moored alongside with the derrick at its maximum working range over the side and with the ship floating at its minimum draught.

4.7.5. The number of complete turns remaining on the drum

of a winch when the complete working length of rope has been paid out should be not less than—

(*a*) three in the case of an ungrooved drum; and

(*b*) two in the case of a grooved drum;

provided that—

(*c*) one turn should remain on the drum in the case of a ship's derrick or ship's crane when it is stowed in its crutches or in its lowest stowed position;

(*d*) two in the case of a ship's derrick when the boom is in its lowest stowed position;

(*e*) three in the case of a mobile crane when the jib is lowered to the horizontal position for removal or insertion of jib sections; and

(*f*) three in the case of a stiff-leg derrick when the jib is in its lowest stowed position.

4.7.6. When a rope is reeled on to a grooved drum—

(*a*) the grooves should be so formed that—

   (i) the radius of the groove exceeds that of the rope by at least 10 per cent;

   (ii) the clearance between adjacent turns of the rope is adequate; and

   (iii) the contour at the bottom of the grooves is circular for a segment subtended by an angle of not less than 120°; and

(*b*) where the grooves have sides, they should be flared as necessary.

4.8. Rope anchorage

4.8.1. (1) The end of the rope should be effectively secured to the drum in a manner that will not damage any part of the rope.

(2) Fibre rope fastenings should not be used for this purpose.

4.9. Derrick interlock

4.9.1. When a derrick is fitted with a common motor for raising or lowering either the jib or the load and the jib is held by a pawl engaging in the derricking drum when the motor is being used to raise or lower a load, an effective interlock should be fitted to the pawl engagement gear so that the pawl cannot be disengaged from the drum until the motor has been positively connected to the derricking drum drive.

4.10. Speed change gear

4.10.1. When a speed change gear is fitted to a winch and is of such a type that the hoisting drum is free to rotate when the change gear is in a neutral position—

(*a*) an emergency brake complying with the requirements of section 4.4 should be fitted to the drum side of the change gears; and

(*b*) the change gear mechanism should be provided with an effective locking device to prevent the gears from becoming accidentally disengaged whilst the winch is hoisting or lowering.

4.11. Limit switches

4.11.1. Every shore crane, and where practicable every shipboard crane or derrick crane, should be provided with properly designed limit switches to limit, as may be appropriate—

(*a*) the raising and lowering motion of the hoist rope;

(*b*) the derricking-in and derricking-out of the jib;

(*c*) the horizontal movement in either direction of the trolley or crab;

(*d*) the slewing motion where this cannot take place through 360°; and

(*e*) the movement of a crane along its track.

4.11.2. Every limit switch should be positively actuated and be so fitted and wired that it fails safe.

4.11.3. After it has been actuated, the limit switch should not prevent motion in the reverse direction.

4.11.4. A crane operator should not be permitted to use and should not use any limit switch as a normal means of stopping the particular motion controlled by that switch.

4.11.5. Where a device is provided to enable a limit switch to be bypassed (for example, to allow the jib of a crane to be lowered to a horizontal position for such purposes as maintenance or changing its length), that device should normally be kept locked against nisuse.

4.11.6. Limit switches should—

(*a*) in the case of an appliance or part of an appliance the movement of which is limited by positive stops, be so positioned that they cut off power to the particular motion before the stops are contacted;

(*b*) in the case of a hoist rope, cut off power sufficiently in advance to prevent any splice in the rope from passing on to the pulley;

(*c*) be rechecked after a new wire rope has been fitted and used for a while, in order to ensure that rope stretch has not caused the limit of movement to be altered.

4.12. Automatic overload cut-outs

4.12.1. (1) Every lifting appliance other than a ship's derrick or derrick crane should, when practicable, be fitted with a device that automatically cuts off the power supply if the load being raised or lowered exceeds the safe working load by a predetermined amount which, in general, should be not less than 103 per cent or more than 110 per cent of the safe working load, or an amount established by the competent national authority.

(2) The cut-out device should not prevent motion in the reverse direction after it is actuated.

(3) In no circumstances should the operator of the appliance be permitted to use the overload cut-out as a normal means of determining the load that can be lifted or lowered.

4.13. Indicator of safe working load

4.13.1. Every lifting appliance having a single safe working load should have that safe working load marked on it.

4.13.2. If a crane has a derricking jib of fixed length, or a horizontal jib upon which a trolley or crab moves so that the safe working load varies according to the radius of the load or trolley or crab, the crane should be fitted with a radius load indicator clearly visible to the driver and indicating—

(*a*) the safe working load of the crane corresponding to the radius of the hook or other lifting attachment on the hoist rope; and

(*b*) the limits of the angular movement of the jib or the longitudinal movement of the trolley or crab, as the case may be—

provided that an indicator need not be fitted in cases in which a rating chart is posted in the cab.

4.13.3. Every crane having a variable radius should bear a marking on its chassis indicating the point from which the radius is measured. The actual radius of the hook or other lifting attachment should be measured with the makers' specified safe working load suspended clear of the ground in order to allow for such factors as deflection of the crane chassis and jib, or rope stretch.

4.13.4. Rating indications should be given as follows:

(*a*) if the safe working load is not greater than 1 tonne, the indications should be in kilograms (kg),

(*b*) if the safe working load is greater than 1 tonne, the indications should be in tonnes (t),

(*c*) every value of safe working load should be marked to one place of decimals except for the values 0.25 and 0.75 and where the figure in the first decimal place is a zero.

4.14. Crane level device

4.14.1. Every crane mobile on the road and every ship's crane should be fitted with a device to indicate to the driver—

(*a*) whether the crane is level or not; and

(*b*) in the case of a ship's crane designed to operate under certain conditions of list or trim, the limits of operation.

4.15. Precautions against high wind

4.15.1. Any crane to be used in an exposed position such that the effect of wind may be detrimental to the safety of the crane should have been designed to have the stability and structural strength required to stand up to the additional stresses involved in—

(*a*) operating normally up to the design wind speed; and

(*b*) withstanding under out-of-service conditions the foreseeable wind speed for the location.

4.15.2. In determining the operating conditions, the effect of the wind upon a load of large superficial area suspended from the crane should be taken into consideration.

4.15.3. In determining the out-of-service conditions, the effect of the strength and duration of gusting should be taken into consideration.

4.15.4. (1) A crane that travels on rails and is of such a size as to render it liable to be blown along the rails under the effect of the wind force should be fitted with devices to enable it to be anchored or secured.

(2) Such devices may be attached to the track, provided that the latter has been designed to allow such attachment.

(3) Where the arrangement provides for separate anchorage points, there should be a sufficient number of them, spaced uniformly along the track, to ensure that a crane will not have to traverse an appreciable distance before it can be anchored.

4.15.5. Wind speed indicators should be fitted at suitable positions on—

(*a*) dockside cranes specially designed for loading and unloading freight containers;

(*b*) ore unloading and similar types of transporters;

(*c*) cranes having slewing horizontal jibs; and

(*d*) any other cranes that are liable to be blown along their rails by high winds—

provided that cranes of types (*c*) and (*d*) need not comply with these requirements if operating on a dock which—

(*a*) either has its own central wind-recording system or has an arrangement to receive early warning signals from a recognised meteorological station in the area; and

(*b*) has an effective system for conveying warnings to the drivers by visual and audible means.

4.15.6. A wind speed indicator fitted to a crane should give visual and audible warning to the driver in the cabin when the wind exceeds a predetermined level.

4.15.7. When the wind speed reaches the predetermined level for a period of sufficient duration to actuate the audible warning device of the wind speed indicator, every crane affected should be immediately taken out of service, and—

(*a*) the crane should be secured by means of its anchoring or securing devices;

(*b*) in addition, in the case of a horizontal jib crane, the jib should be released so that it can freely weather-vane; and

(*c*) in the case of a transporter crane, any arm that is spanning a ship being loaded or unloaded by the crane at the time should be retracted.

4.16. Transporters

4.16.1. In cases in which the driver's cabin is attached to and travels with the crab, the cabin suspension gear should be so designed that if the cabin or the crab is accidentally displaced from its rails the cabin cannot fall from the transporter arm.

4.16.2. In any cases in which the arm of a transporter has to operate in close proximity to any part of a ship's superstructure and the ship is apt to surge under the influence of such factors as tide, swell or wind, a signaller in radio or telephone communication with the driver should be stationed at a suitable position in order to alert the driver in the event of danger.

4.16.3. (1) The lifting frame of a freight container transporter crane should be fitted with devices which give the driver a visual indication whether the twist locks are or are not properly engaged in the corner fittings of the freight container being handled.

(2) Where practicable, the devices should automatically cut out the hoisting motion if one of the locks is not properly engaged.

4.16.4. A means of emergency escape from the driver's cabin should be provided and periodically inspected for serviceability.

4.16.5. No action affecting the operation of crane machinery should be taken without the knowledge of the driver.

4.17. Operator's cabin

4.17.1. The operator's cabin of a lifting appliance should—

(*a*) afford the operator adequate protection against the weather, including the sun where necessary;

(*b*) afford the operator an adequate view of the area of operation;

(*c*) afford the operator ready access to his operating position and, where necessary, to working parts in the cabin;

(*d*) be adequately heated in cold weather by means that do not emit noxious or objectionable fumes;

(*e*) be adequately ventilated, either artificially or mechanically, according to the local conditions;

(*f*) have windows capable of being readily and safely cleaned inside and out;

(*g*) have a comfortable and purpose-designed seat (particularly where the operator is constantly looking downwards), and foot rests where necessary;

(*h*) in the case of an elevated cabin, have a sliding or inwards-opening door that can be readily opened from both inside and outside;

(*i*) be of fire-proof construction;

(*j*) be provided with fire extinguishers of a type suited to the confined space of the cabin and the proximity of electrical apparatus;

(*k*) be so designed that noise and vibration remain within acceptable limits; and

(*l*) have an operator's position and seat properly protected from excessive heat emanating from the driving mechanism.

4.18. Swivels

4.18.1. A swivel should be fitted between the hoist rope and the hook or other lifting attachment, and except in the case of a ship's derrick the swivel should be fitted with ball-bearings or roller bearings that can be regularly lubricated.

4.19. Overhauling weight

4.19.1. Where an overhauling weight is fitted at the end of a hoist rope—

(*a*) it should be of a design that will minimise the danger of its catching on any part of a hold, ship's superstructure or similar obstruction;

(*b*) where practicable, it should be connected to the rope by means of a short length of chain and the weight and swivel fitted to the chain;

(*c*) where it is necessary to fit the weight directly on to the rope, the hole in the weight should be machine-bored and bell-mouthed at each end and the rope should be served where in contact with the weight; and

(*d*) except in a case in which the weight is attached to a chain, the weight should be constructed in two halves to facilitate examination of the rope, and the two halves should be secured by at least four countersunk bolts, the nuts of which are fitted with suitable locking devices.

4.20. Crane tracks

4.20.1. The track of a travelling crane should—

(*a*) be of adequate section, properly laid, firm and level, of adequate bearing capacity and have an even running surface;

(*b*) if used for anchoring the crane against crane movement under high wind,[1] be designed for that purpose; and

(*c*) where used by an electrically driven crane, be properly electrically bonded and earthed.

4.21. Contact rail channels

4.21.1. A channel on the dock side containing electric contact rails for cranes should be—

(*a*) properly drained; and

(*b*) designed to prevent from entering the channel any article of a size, or waste material of a volume, likely to cause danger.

4.22. Obstacle clearances

4.22.1. At any place where a track-mounted crane passes an obstacle, including stacked goods or a vehicle being loaded or unloaded—

(*a*) where practicable, a clearance of not less than 90 cm should be arranged between the crane and the obstacle;

---

[1] See paragraph 4.15.4.

(*b*) a permanently fixed obstacle should, so far as is practicable, comply with the requirements of paragraph 2.1.5;

(*c*) if goods are permanently stacked near a crane track, boundary lines for the stacking of goods should be conspicuously and permanently marked on the ground; and

(*d*) where it is not practicable at any time and at any place to provide and maintain the clearance required under (*a*) above, effective steps should be taken to prevent the access of any person to such a place at such a time.

4.23. Track clearance

4.23.1. (1) So far as is practicable, the track of a track-mounted crane should be kept clear, in particular of loose material and rubbish.

(2) The crane chassis should be so designed as to clear automatically the rails of dunnage and similar material as the crane moves.

4.24. Audible warning alarms

4.24.1. (1) A transporter, portal or similar crane should be fitted at ground level with an audible alarm that sounds when the crane begins to move and that is sufficiently loud to be heard by anyone working in the vicinity.

(2) The crane should be fitted with a horn or similar warning device that can be operated separately by the driver to warn or attract the attention of any person within the operational area of the crane.

4.25. Guards

4.25.1. Suitable guards should be fitted to guard—

(*a*) the track wheels of any rail-mounted crane at ground level in such a manner as to prevent danger to any person's feet; and (*b*) the winding drum, if any, for the crane's flexible power cable, unless the drum is so placed as to be as safe as if it were guarded.

4.26. Buffers

4.26.1. (1) Adequate buffers or stops should be fitted at each end of the track to reduce the danger of crane derailment to a minimum.

(2) If more than one crane is located and operated on the same track or more than one trolley on the same bridge, they should be equipped with buffers at their facing ends.

(3) Buffers need not be fitted where automatic means of preventing contact are installed.

4.27. Crane chassis

4.27.1. The chassis should be so designed that in the event of breakage of a wheel, failure of an axle or derailment it will prevent collapse or overturning of the crane.

4.28. Tyres

4.28.1. (1) Where a lifting appliance travels on wheels with pneumatic tyres the tyres should be—

(*a*) free from any defect; and

(*b*) maintained at the correct tyre pressure.

(2) The correct tyre pressure should be conspicuously marked on the chassis near each wheel.

4.29. Steam winches

4.29.1. Winches operated by steam power should be so constructed and installed that—

(*a*) dockworkers will not be scalded by hot water or steam; and (*b*) steam from the exhaust pipes will not obscure the operator's field of vision.

4.29.2. It should be possible to lock the reversing control lever in the neutral position.

4.29.3. The stop valve between each winch and the deck steam line should be close to the winch and easily accessible at all times, and should turn with normal hand pressure.

4.29.4. Valve handles should be insulated by suitable material.

4.29.5. A constant steam pressure should be maintained at the winches to ensure safety and smooth working while the winches are in operation.

4.30. Cargo platforms

4.30.1. Cargo platforms (except those formed by cargo itself) should be made of sound material, substantially and firmly constructed, adequately supported and, where necessary, securely fastened, and maintained in good repair.

4.30.2. Platforms should not be overloaded.

4.30.3. Hatch covers should not be used in the construction of platforms.

4.30.4. Cargo platforms should—

(*a*) be of sufficient size to receive cargo and to ensure the safety of persons working on them;

(*b*) if of a height exceeding 1.5 m, be protected, on any side which is not being used for receiving or delivering cargo, by fencing complying with the relevant requirements of paragraph 2.4.1; and

(*c*) be provided with safe means of access, such as ladders or stairs.

4.30.5. Portable trestles should be so placed as to be steady.

4.31. Conveyors

4.31.1. Conveyors should be of sound material, of good construction and of sufficient strength to support safely the loads for which they are intended, and should be kept in good repair.

4.31.2. (1) Conveying machinery should be so constructed and installed as to avoid hazardous points between moving and stationary parts or objects.

(2) When a passageway is adjacent to an open conveyor, a clearance of at least 1 m should be provided.

4.31.3. When workers have to cross over conveyors, regular crossing facilities, adequately lighted and affording safe passage, should be provided if necessary to prevent danger.

4.31.4. When conveyors that are not entirely enclosed cross over places where workers are employed or might pass beneath them, sheet or screen guards should be provided to catch any material which might fall from the conveyors.

4.31.5. Power-driven conveyors should be provided at loading and unloading stations, at drive and take-up ends and if necessary at other convenient places with devices for stopping the conveyor machinery in an emergency.

4.31.6. Adequate fencing should be provided at transfer points.

4.31.7. Conveyors which carry loads up inclines should be provided with mechanical devices that will prevent machinery from reversing and carrying the loads back towards the loading point if the power is cut off.

4.31.8. Where two or more conveyors are operated together, the controlling devices should be so arranged that no conveyor can feed on to a stopped conveyor.

4.31.9. Where the tops of hoppers for feeding conveyors are less than 90 cm above the floors, the openings should be adequately guarded.

4.31.10. (1) Where conveyors extend to points not visible from the control stations, they should be equipped with gongs, whistles or signal lights to be used by the operators before starting the machinery so as to warn workers who might be in positions of danger.

(2) Similar measures should be taken where necessary to enable the workers to communicate with the operator.

(3) When any dockworker is attending a conveyor, the conveyor should be provided with an emergency trip wire or other effective stopping device operable throughout the length of the conveyor.

4.31.11. Suitable provision should be made for the safe cleaning of conveyors and for clearing obstructions.

4.31.12. Conveyors should be provided with automatic and continuous lubrication systems or with lubricating facilities so arranged that the oilers can oil and grease the machinery without coming within dangerous proximity to moving parts.

4.31.13. Conveyors should be thoroughly inspected at suitable intervals.

4.31.14. Dockworkers should not ride on conveyors.

4.31.15. Belt conveyors should be provided with guards at the nips of belts and drums.

4.31.16. Intake openings of blowers or exhaust fans for pneumatic conveyors should be protected with substantial metal screens or gratings.

4.32. Gravity rollers, chutes and dray ladders

4.32.1. Gravity rollers, chutes and dray ladders should—

(*a*) be of sound material, good construction and sufficient strength to support safely the loads for which they are intended; and

(*b*) be maintained in good repair.

4.32.2. The frames of gravity rollers, chutes and dray ladders should be kept free of splinters, sharp edges and rough surfaces.

4.32.3. Gravity rollers, chutes and dray ladders should not be used for the passage of persons.

4.32.4. The rolls of gravity rollers should be kept locked in position to prevent them from falling or jumping out of the frame.

4.32.5. The frames of gravity rollers should be equipped with hand grips.

4.32.6. When necessary, provision should be made for braking objects at the delivery end of the roller.

4.32.7. The side boards of chutes should be of sufficient height to prevent cargo from falling off.

4.32.8. The ends of chutes should be equipped with adequate securing devices.

4.32.9. At the top end of each upright, dray ladders should be provided with an adequate securing device so that they cannot slip.

4.32.10. Rolling goods should be moved only with two ropes, or with safety appliances.

5. Mobile cranes[1]

5.1. Outriggers

5.1.1. Where a mobile crane is fitted with outriggers—

(*a*) when in use, the outriggers should be fully extended and locked in position;

(*b*) the jacks should be extended sufficiently to take the load fully off the wheels; and

(*c*) unless the crane is on firm ground such as concrete, the jacks should rest upon adequate and suitable packing.

5.2. Ballast

5.2.1. In cases in which the amount of ballast fitted to a mobile crane depends upon the length of the jib, measures should be taken to ensure that the crane has been properly ballasted before use.

5.3. Jibs or booms of variable length

5.3.1. In cases in which a mobile crane is fitted with a jib or boom of a length that can be varied by the insertion or removal of a jib or boom section, the following precautions should be taken when the jib or boom is lowered for its length to be changed:

(*a*) where necessary, the automatic safe load indicator provided in accordance with the requirements of section 5.7 should be disconnected;

(*b*) the jib or boom should be lowered along the fore-and-aft axis of the crane and deposited upon a sufficient number of blocks each of adequate strength and suitably spaced; and

[1] The provisions of this chapter, in addition to any applicable provisions of Chapter 4, apply to all mobile cranes.

(*c*) extreme care should be taken when releasing the bolts of a section since the jib or boom may collapse unless it is adequately supported.

5.3.2. (1) No section should be inserted unless it—

(*a*) has been previously tested in accordance with the requirements of Appendix A;

(*b*) is marked for the correct position in the jib;

(*c*) is free from any patent defect, particularly distortion; and

(*d*) fits readily and does not require undue force to position or secure it.

(2) Only boom or jib sections intended for use with the particular crane should be used.

5.4. Travelling with load

5.4.1. For mobile cranes designed to travel with loads suspended—

(*a*) the rating of the crane should be determined when it is free on its wheels;

(*b*) the jib should lie in the direction of the fore-and-aft axis of the crane;

(*c*) the jib should be derricked out as far as possible to the point where the load carried is equal to or slightly below the safe working load of the crane with the jib in that position;

(*d*) the load should be just sufficiently clear of the ground to ensure that it does not touch the ground under bounce of the jib;

(*e*) if the load is of awkward size, guidelines should be attached to keep it steady, particularly on a windy day; and

(*f*) the acceleration and braking of the crane should be as gentle as possible.

5.5. Trapping of workers

5.5.1. To prevent workers from being trapped—

(1) Alternating black and yellow stripes should be painted between the slewing part of the mobile crane and the side of the fixed part of the chassis over which it slews, and—

(*a*) before slewing, the operator should, where possible, ensure that no person is in that trapping area; or

(*b*) where the precaution advocated in (*a*) above is not possible, another person should be suitably positioned to ensure that either no persons are in the trapping area or, if persons are in the trapping area, that they are in contact with the driver.

(2) No part of the crane should go closer than 1 m to any fixed obstruction unless it has been ascertained that no person is in the vicinity.

(3) No person, especially no slinger, should be between the load and an adjacent fixed obstacle, since owing to deflection of the jib and tilt of the crane the load is likely to move horizontally for a short distance when it is first lifted.

(4) Unless permanently guarded, the access area within the swing radius of the outermost part of the body of a revolving crane should be temporarily guarded by taut ropes or other suitable means so as to prevent dockworkers from being in a position to be caught between the chassis of the crane and other stationary objects or the crane itself.

5.6. Depositing of load

5.6.1. A load should not be deposited heavily.[1]

5.7. Safe load indicators

5.7.1. (1) A crane that is mobile on the road and fitted with a

[1] Since the sling may jump from the hook and in certain circumstances dangerous backlash of the crane may result.

derricking jib of a length that may be varied either by the insertion or removal of jib sections or by telescoping should be fitted with—

(*a*) an indicator which by itself or in combination with tables posted in the cabin enables the driver to determine the safe working load under any combination of use of the crane; and

(*b*) an automatic safe load indicator which should, unless national regulations or standards provide otherwise—

  (i) give a clear visual warning to the driver of the crane when the load carried by the crane is within the range of 90 per cent to 97 per cent of the crane's safe working load at any particular radius of the hook, angle of the jib to the horizontal, length of the jib or combination of any of these; and

  (ii) give a clear and distinctive audible warning to the driver and any other person working in the immediate vicinity of the crane when the load being carried by the crane is within the range of 103 per cent to 110 per cent in excess of the crane's safe working load at any particular radius of the hook, angle of the jib to the horizontal, length of jib or any combination of these.

(2) The indicators should be fitted with means for adjustment to suit the various methods of use of the crane, such as when the crane is free on its wheels, supported by stabilising spreaders or fitted with a fly boom.

5.8. Tandem lift

5.8.1. Mobile cranes should be used in tandem lift only when other means are not available; when mobile cranes are so used the precautions recommended in this section should be taken.

5.8.2. The operation should be under the direct supervision of a competent person, and the method of operation should be carefully planned in advance.

5.8.3. The load on each crane should be calculated, and kept at least 25 per cent below the safe working load. The weight of the slings or any special lifting gear such as a lifting beam should be included in the weight of the load.

5.8.4. The jib of each crane should be derricked as high as is practicable in order to obtain the greatest length of wire rope between the load and the jib head.

5.8.5. (1) The cranes should be so positioned that the crane ropes are vertical.

(2) The load should be raised no higher above the ground than is necessary, and if at any time movement of the hoist ropes out of the vertical becomes perceptible the movement of the load in the direction producing that movement should be halted.

5.8.6. The load should be held by a sufficient number of guide ropes to damp down any tendency for the load to swing.

5.8.7. When it is necessary to lower the load to the ground, this should be done slowly and gently, and if the ground surface is hard persons should be standing by to insert packing pieces between the load and the ground wherever necessary to avoid sling damage.

5.8.8. (1) All motions should be carried out smoothly and at low speed.

(2) If slewing cannot be avoided, particular attention should be paid to preventing one crane from exerting a side force on the jib of the other.

5.8.9. Should the load have a large surface/weight ratio, the operations should not be carried out in a high wind or during gusting.

5.8.10. Where loads are regularly required to be moved by tandem lifting—

(*a*) where practicable, special gear for producing equal tension on the hoist ropes should be employed;

(*b*) the weight of the load together with the position of its centre of gravity should be marked on the load or otherwise indicated by the consignor;

(*c*) the load should, if practicable, be fitted with special lifting attachments so placed that each crane is suitably loaded; and

(*d*) the cranes should perform only one motion at a time.

5.9. Side loading

5.9.1. No jib or boom of a mobile crane should be deliberately side-loaded.

5.10. Use aboard vessels

5.10.1. Mobile cranes placed for use aboard barges or other vessels should be positively secured to the vessel unless the effect of the use of the crane aboard the vessel and the nature of the vessel itself are such that there is no list or change of trim of a magnitude endangering the stability of the crane.

5.10.2. If a mobile crane aboard a vessel is not permanently attached to the vessel, and is fitted with outriggers, they should be used whenever the crane is being operated.

5.10.3. If a mobile crane is permanently located in a particular place aboard a vessel, it should be attached to the vessel by permanent means.

5.10.4. When a mobile crane is to be used aboard a barge or other vessel, the crane manufacturer, or if his services are not available the agency testing, examining and certificating the crane, or a qualified engineer acceptable to the national authority, should be consulted for any changes to the crane ratings which may be necessary owing to list or a change of trim of the barge or other vessel. The reduced ratings should be posted in accordance with the requirements of paragraph 4.13.4 and should not be exceeded.

6. Ship's cargo pulley blocks (wire rope)

6.1. Single-sheave blocks

6.1.1. The safe working load of a single-sheave cargo block is the maximum load that can be safely lifted by that block when it is suspended by its head fitting and the load is secured to a wire rope passing round its sheave.[1]

6.1.2. When a single-sheave cargo block is so rigged that the load to be lifted is secured to its head fitting, the block being suspended by the wire rope passing round its sheave,[2] it should be permissible to lift a load twice the value of the safe working load marked on the block in accordance with the requirements of paragraph 6.1.1.

6.1.3. The safe working load of a single-sheave cargo block incorporated elsewhere in a derrick rig so that it is secured by its head fitting and subjected to tension arising from a wire rope that forms part of the derrick rig and passes round or partially round the sheave is half of the resultant load upon its head fitting, due allowance being made for the effects of friction in the block and rope stiffness (i.e. the extra load arising from the effort of bending the wire rope partially round the sheave).

6.1.4. The proof test load applied to a single-sheave block should not be less than that indicated in Appendix paragraph D.2.1.

6.2. Multi-sheave blocks

6.2.1. The safe working load of a multi-sheave block is the maximum force that may be applied to its head fitting. In practice this is the value of the resultant tension upon it when it is rigged in the derrick, due allowance being made for the effects of friction in the block and rope stiffness.[3]

---

[1] See Appendix H, figure 1 and Appendix paragraph H.2.2.

[2] See Appendix H, figure 2.

[3] See Appendix H.

6.2.2. The proof test load applied to a multi-sheaved block should not be less than that given in Appendix paragraph D.2.1.

6.3. Rigging

6.3.1. Cargo blocks should be rigged in accordance with the rigging plan required under section 7.1 and with the requirements of sections 6.1 and 6.2, in order to ensure that the block is properly matched for the load or tension that will be applied to it when in use.

6.4. Design

6.4.1. Every block should comply with the requirements of section 4.2.

6.4.2. The block design should be based upon a wire rope having a tensile strength of 130–160 kg/mm^2 (83–102 tonnes/in^2) and a coefficient of utilisation in accordance with the requirements of Appendix E; provided that a block used solely on a ship's heavy lift derrick may be designed for a rope having a tensile strength in excess of those figures.

6.4.3. The diameter of the sheave (measured at the bottom of the rope groove) should not be less than 14 times the diameter of the rope for which the block has been designed.

6.4.4. The depth of the groove should preferably be equal to the rope diameter, and should in any event not be less than three-quarters of that diameter. The bottom of the groove should have a circular contour over a segment subtended by an angle of not less than 120°, the radius of the groove exceeding that of the rope by at least 10 per cent. The sides of the groove should be slightly flared and the inside edge of the rim radiused.

6.4.5. End and partition plates should—

(*a*) where flame-cut from plate, have their edges smoothed off;

(*b*) have through holes for axle pin, bolts and other parts machined and in true alignment;

(*c*) be of such a size that their edges project beyond the sheave or sheaves to give ample protection to the rope; and

(*d*) have a clearance of not less than 2 mm between them and the sheave.

6.4.6. Lightening holes should be provided in sheaves only if the end plates are solid.

6.4.7. (1) The axle pin should—

(*a*) be fitted in such a way as to prevent the pin from turning; and

(*b*) if fitted with a screwed nut, be designed to tighten against a shoulder on the pin instead of tending to squeeze the plates together, and be provided with a suitable locking device.

(2) The assembly of the axle pin and swivel head fitting should be of such a design as to permit the block to be completely dismantled when necessary for thorough examination.

6.4.8. Suitable greasing points should be provided, and the greasing nipples should be so placed that they are not liable to be damaged and that the block can be greased when the block is in the derrick rig.

6.4.9. Where any part of a block, such as the axle pin or head fitting, is made of high-tensile or alloy steel, it should be marked in accordance with the requirements of Appendix F.

6.4.10. A cargo block fitted to the heel of a derrick for the cargo runner or hoist rope should be provided with a duck bill or similar type of head designed to restrict the downward movement of the block when the runner becomes slack.

6.4.11. A cargo block fitted to the head of a derrick should, when used in union purchase, and in other cases where practicable, be fitted with an eye, preferably of the swivelling type.

6.4.12. Every cargo block should be tested and thoroughly examined in accordance with the requirements of Appendices B and C.

6.4.13. A cargo block should be fitted with an irremovable plate bearing the following information:

(*a*) its safe working load in tonnes and decimals of a tonne to the first decimal place except for 0.25 and 0.75;

(*b*) an identification mark to relate the block to its certificate of test and examination;

(*c*) where appropriate, an identification mark corresponding to its position on the ship's rigging plan;

(*d*) the diameter of the wire rope for which it has been designed; and

(*e*) whether any part is made of special steel.

6.5. Care and maintenance

6.5.1. When a block is inspected, it should be ascertained that—

(*a*) no sheave is cracked at the rim, and no part of the rim is missing;

(*b*) the groove is not excessively worn;

(*c*) the sheave or sheaves turn(s) freely and smoothly;

(*d*) the head fitting swivel is securely fastened and free from visible defects, and the shank is not distorted and turns freely by hand and is not slack in its hole;

(*e*) clearance between the sheaves and partition or side plates is not excessive;

(*f*) the side straps are sound and in particular free from any cracks;

(*g*) the greasing arrangement is satisfactory; and

(*h*) the plate required under paragraph 6.4.13 is intact and the information thereon is legible.

6.5.2. (1) For a thorough examination in accordance with the requirements of subparagraph 4.2.1(*e*) and Appendix paragraph C.1.1, a block should be stripped down.

(2) The head swivel fitting and axle pin should be checked to

ascertain that they are free from any hairline cracks, particularly at the termination of the thread and at any change of section.

(3) If any sheave is fitted with a bush bearing, it should be ascertained that the bush is not worn and is secure against turning relative to the sheave boss.

(4) If any sheave is fitted with roller bearings or ball-bearings, it should be ascertained that they are still tight in the sheave boss. Only the axle pin need be withdrawn for the examination if it has been ascertained that the bearings are not tight. If it comes free from the bearing too readily, the pin should be changed.

(5) Straps and any welding securing the straps to bridge pieces (traverses) should be checked for any hairline cracks.

(6) Lubrication holes should be checked to ascertain that they are clear.

6.5.3. A block should—

(*a*) not be subjected to any form of heat treatment;

(*b*) not be dropped from a height;

(*c*) be regularly lubricated;

(*d*) not have its plate [1] or any grease nipple painted over; and

(*e*) be kept in the ship's cargo store when not in use.

---

[1] See paragraph 6.4.13.

7. Ship's derricks

7.1. Rigging plans

7.1.1. Every ship should carry adequate rigging plans showing at least—

(*a*) the correct position of guys;

(*b*) the resultant force on blocks and guys;

(*c*) the position of blocks;

(*d*) their identification marking; and

(*e*) arrangements for union purchase.

7.2. Slewing guys

7.2.1. Slewing guys should be designed for operation of the derrick with the ship having a list of not more than 5° and a trim of not more than 2° with the derrick at its maximum outreach.

7.3. Span winch

7.3.1. (1) A derrick other than one that has its own power-operated topping winch should be provided, whenever this is reasonably practicable, with a span winch complying with the relevant requirements of Chapter 8.

(2) Where this is not reasonably practicable, a span chain joined to the span rope by means of a monkey or a delta plate should be employed.

7.4. Temporary stopper

7.4.1. No derrick should be rigged and adjusted for angle otherwise than by its own power-operated topping winch or by a span winch complying with the relevant requirements of Chapter 8. It should be prohibited to use a short length of chain shackled to the deck and hitched to the span rope, which is held by hand at the other end, as a temporary stopper.

7.5. Heel block

7.5.1. The derrick heel block should comply with the requirements of paragraph 6.4.10, and the block fitted to the head of the derrick should comply with those of paragraph 6.4.11.

7.6. Rigging

7.6.1. When a derrick is being rigged—

(*a*) a man should always be stationed at each span winch and/or cargo winch in use;

(*b*) only persons engaged in the actual rigging work should be allowed in the vicinity of the derrick; provided that other persons may pass along the deck if the person in charge of the rigging announces that it is safe for them to do so;

(*c*) the wire rope should be checked to ensure that it is free from corrosion, kinks, needling or any other patent defects;

(*d*) shackles securing all blocks should be fitted in the correct way, and have their pins properly tightened;

(*e*) block sheaves should be checked to ensure that they are free to turn and are properly lubricated;

(*f*) guys, including preventer guys where appropriate, should be properly attached to the derrick head and particularly to the correct deck eye plates;[1]

(*g*) the goose neck should be checked to ascertain that it is free to swivel (this may be done when the derrick is at a low angle—

---

[1] To avoid the possible danger of jack-knifing, that is to say a situation in which the head of the derrick rises, when in use, in an uncontrolled manner even though the load is suspended.

30° to 50°—with one or more men gently swinging on the guys); and

(*h*) in the case of a heavy lift derrick, a check should be made to ascertain that any temporary mast or samson post stays are properly fitted and that any special slewing guys which are directly attached to the lower cargo block are properly rigged.

7.6.2. When a ship is carrying deck cargo stowed in such a manner that the deck eye plates are inaccessible—

(*a*) the guys should be secured to wire rope or chain pendants designed specially for the purpose and of sufficient length to enable the guys to be coupled to the pendants at the top level of the deck cargo; and

(*b*) extreme care should be taken to ensure that the relative positions of the guys as shown on the rigging plans are not disturbed.[1]

7.6.3. A derrick should not be rigged at an angle lower than the angle marked upon it in accordance with the requirements of paragraph 7.8.3.

7.7. Use in union purchase

7.7.1. (1) When a derrick is to be used in union purchase—

(*a*) a preventer guy should be fitted in addition to the main guy (in this connection care should be taken not to confuse a guy intended only for trimming a boom with a working guy);

(*b*) the preventer and the main guy should be attached to deck eye plates that are separate but placed as close together as is practicable;

(*c*) the preventer and the main guy should be adjusted when the derrick boom is under a slight dynamic loading (with a heavy hatch beam suspended, for example); and

[1] Since otherwise there may be a considerable danger that the derricks will jack-knife.

(*d*) the main (working) guy should be under slightly more tension than the preventer guy.

(2) Where the means of adjusting the length of a guy consists of—

(*a*) a claw device used in conjunction with a series of metal ferrules compressed to a wire rope secured to a deck eye plate, the claw should be of suitable design and of adequate strength and be so arranged that it will not be accidentally released in the event of temporary partial slackness in the guy; and

(*b*) a fibre block and tackle, a rope of man-made fibre should be used.[1]

(3) The hoist ropes of the two derricks should be secured to a common ring (also carrying the cargo hook) by means of suitable swivels.

(4) The hook should be fitted as close to the junction of the falls as possible.

7.7.2. When derricks are in use in union purchase—

(*a*) the angle between the two cargo falls should not exceed 120° at any time;

(*b*) the load should be raised only sufficiently to clear the coaming, bulwark or railings, whichever is the highest; and

(*c*) slings on loads should be of minimum length to enable the height of lift to be kept as low as possible.

7.8. Marking of safe working load

7.8.1. Each derrick should be legibly marked with its safe working load as follows—

(*a*) when the derrick is used only in single purchase, "SWL *x* t";

(*b*) when the derrick is used additionally with a lower cargo block, "SWL *x*/*x* t"; and

---

[1] Because it has better elasticity and does not need adjustment when it becomes wet or dry.

(*c*) when the derrick is used in union purchase, "SWL (U)xt" where x=safe working load.

7.8.2. (1) The letters and numbers should not be less than 77 mm high.

(2) They should be painted either a light colour on a dark background or a dark colour on a light background.

7.8.3. The lowest angle to the horizontal that the derrick may be used should also be marked on the derrick in the manner described in paragraph 7.8.2.

8. Derrick span gear (topping lift) winches

8.1. Driven by adjacent winch[1]

8.1.1. (1) A derrick span gear winch driven by a rope whip from an adjacent power-driven winch should have two separate drums, one for the rope whip and the other for the derrick span rope, or a single drum divided into two parts by a substantial flange of sufficient depth to ensure effective separation of the ropes.

(2) The winch should be fitted with sprockets on each side of the drum or part of the drum containing the span rope, as well as with pawls cross-connected in such a manner that they engage into the sprockets simultaneously.

(3) The sprockets should be of such a shape that the pawls tend to engage harder when under load.

(4) The pawl-operating gear should be fitted with suitable hand-holds to enable the pawls to be engaged or disengaged safely.

(5) The pawls and sprockets should be designed to be capable of resisting a torque not less than 1.5 times the maximum torque induced by the derrick when it is in conditions of maximum resultant force.

(6) The winch should bear a plate in a conspicuous position containing the following information:

(*a*) the direction of rotation of the drum when the derrick is being raised;

(*b*) the size of wire rope for which it has been designed;

(*c*) the working length of wire rope it has been designed to accommodate;

(*d*) particulars of its identity; and

(*e*) a warning notice to the effect that the derrick must not be topped or raised while it is bearing a load.

---

[1] See also paragraphs 4.2.1(*a*), (*c*), (*d*), 4.7.4, and 4.8.1, which are applicable.

8.2. Topping winch

8.2.1. (1) When a topping winch is used, a person should be standing by the pawl-operating gear ready to engage the pawls as soon as the signal is received from the person hauling in or paying out the rope whip.

(2) No attempt should be made to engage the pawls while the winch drum is rotating in the direction for lowering the derrick.

8.3. Span gear winch

8.3.1. A span gear winch driven from another winch by means of a whip rope should not be used on a derrick having a safe working load (in single fall) exceeding 3 tonnes.

8.4. Span gear whip rope[1]

8.4.1. A whip rope used for driving a span gear winch should—

(*a*) not be used on a drum that due to its condition is liable to damage the rope;

(*b*) not have more turns on the drum than is necessary for safety; provided that extra turns should be made on a drum that is whelped;

(*c*) not be surged or rendered on the drum, particularly in the case of man-made rope;[2]

(*d*) not contain any splice; and

(*e*) be of a suitable size to ensure adequate strength and handling.

---

[1] See also Chapters 9, 10 and 11, which are applicable.

[2] Because frictional heat is apt to damage the rope.

8.5. Operators

8.5.1. The winch operators should—

(*a*) endeavour to arrange the rope to coil on the deck;

(*b*) wear suitable gloves to protect their hands from possible burns; and

(*c*) not stand in any bight of the rope.

9. Wire rope

9.1. Certification

9.1.1. No wire rope should be used unless—

(*a*) it has been made to a recognised national or international standard or alternatively to the requirements of a classification society;

(*b*) it has a guaranteed minimum breaking load certified by the maker; and

(*c*) its construction is suitable for the purpose for which it is used.

9.2. Minimum breaking load

9.2.1. (1) The guaranteed minimum breaking load should not be less than the product of the safe working load and a factor known as the coefficient of utilisation.

(2) The coefficient of utilisation should be determined in accordance with the requirements of Appendix E.

9.3. Galvanised rope

9.3.1. Wire rope used for a ship's derrick should be galvanised in accordance with a recognised national or international standard.

9.4. Paying out

9.4.1. (1) Great care should be taken when a wire rope is paid out from a reel.

(2) The length of rope required for the particular use should be taken from the reel or coil either by mounting the reel or coil on a turntable or by rolling the reel along the dock surface or deck after the latter has been suitably cleaned and cleared as necessary.

(3) The rope should not be allowed to kink or twist about its axis.

(4) The rope should not be taken from the centre of the coil or be allowed to spring off in turns.

(5) Unless the rope is of the preformed type, it should be served or seized before being cut.

9.4.2. Except for eye splices in the ends of wires and for endless rope slings, each wire rope used in hoisting or lowering, or in bulling cargo, should consist of one continuous piece without knot or splice.

9.5. Thimble or loop splice

9.5.1. (1) A thimble or loop splice should have at least three tucks with a whole strand of rope, followed by two tucks with half the wires cut out of each strand.

(2) All tucks other than the first should be against the lay of the rope.

(3) If another form of splice is used, it should be as efficient as that described in subparagraph (1).

9.5.2. A splice in which all the tucks are with the lay of the rope should not be used in the construction of a sling or in any part of a lifting appliance where the rope is apt to twist about its axis.

9.5.3. If a loop is made or a thimble secured to a wire rope by means of a compressed metal ferrule, the ferrule should be made to a manufacturer's standard. In particular—

(*a*) the material used for the manufacture of the ferrule should be suitable, particularly to withstand plastic deformation without any sign of cracking;

(*b*) the correct size (both in diameter and length) of ferrule should be used for the diameter of the rope;

(*c*) the end of the rope where looped back should pass completely through the ferrule;

(*d*) the correct dies should be used for the size of the ferrule;

(*e*) the correct closing or compression pressure should be applied to the dies; and

(*f*) ferrules used on slings should have the end remote from the hook or eye tapered in order to facilitate the withdrawal of the sling from beneath a load.

9.6. Terminal fittings

9.6.1. The terminal fitting of any wire rope should be capable of withstanding—

(*a*) not less than 95 per cent of the minimum breaking load of the rope in the case of a rope of a diameter of 50 mm or less; and

(*b*) not less than 90 per cent in the case of a rope of a diameter above 50 mm.

9.6.2. (1) A wedge socket used as a terminal fitting of a lifting appliance should be suitable for the size of rope and be properly fitted.

(2) The tail should protrude sufficiently from the socket to enable it to be bent back upon itself to form a loop, the end of the tail then being clamped or lashed to the part of the tail emerging from the socket (not clamped to the main part of the rope).

(3) The wedge should be inserted and driven home by gentle hammering with a mallet.

(4) A heavy load (up to the safe working load of the socket if practicable) should be lifted a short distance and then be allowed to descend and be braked normally in order to bed the wedge.

(5) A Langs lay rope should be used only on condition that it is not free to twist about its axis (i.e. both ends of the rope should be secured).

9.6.3. Bolted clamps (such as crosby, plate or bulldog cramps) should not be used to form a terminal join in any hoist rope, derricking rope of guys of a ship's derrick or derrick crane or in the construction of a sling.

9.6.4. A rope made of fibre interspersed with the wire strands should not be used on a lifting appliance.

9.7. Dressing

9.7.1. (1) The wire rope of a lifting appliance, other than the wire rope of a ship's derrick, should be regularly treated with a wire rope dressing free from acid or alkali and whenever possible of a type recommended by the manufacturer.

(2) Where it is practicable and safe to do so, the dressing should be applied where the rope passes over a drum or pulley.[1]

(3) Particular attention should be given to a wire rope that is used in a dusty or abrasive environment; in such an environment it may be necessary to clean the rope thoroughly before applying the new dressing.

9.8. Inspection

9.8.1. The wire rope of a lifting appliance should be inspected and thoroughly examined when in use in accordance with the requirements of Appendix paragraph C.1.4.

9.8.2. The complete length of rope should be inspected and examined in accordance with the requirements of Appendix sub-paragraph C.1.4(2), i.e. including the turns of rope remaining on the drum when the normal working length has been paid out.

9.8.3. If a wire rope contains any grips, wedge sockets or the like, they should be removed during the inspection of the rope.

9.9. Replacement

9.9.1. A wire rope should be replaced—

(*a*) if it shows signs of corrosion, particularly internal corrosion;

---

[1] Because the bending of the rope there facilitates penetration of the dressing.

(*b*) if there is any tendency towards birdcaging (i.e. separation of the strands or wires);

(*c*) if it shows signs of excessive wear indicated by flats appearing on the individual wires;

(*d*) if the number of broken wires or needles in any length of ten diameters exceeds 5 per cent of the total number of wires in the rope;

(*e*) if broken wires—

(i) appear in one strand only;

(ii) are concentrated in a shorter length of rope than ten diameters; or

(iii) appear in the tucks of a splice; or

(*f*) if there is more than one broken wire immediately adjacent to a compressed metal ferrule or any end fitting fitted in accordance with the requirements of paragraph 9.5.3.

9.9.2. The reason for the defects listed in paragraph 9.9.1 should be investigated and remedial action taken.

9.10. Splices

9.10.1 Any splice in a wire rope fitted to a lifting appliance should be protected only at its tail in order to ensure that no deterioration of the splice (i.e. broken wires) will remain unseen.

10. Man-made fibre rope

10.1. Restrictions in use

10.1.1. Rope composed of man-made fibre should not be used for a sling or as part of a lifting appliance unless—

(*a*) the manufacturer has certificated its guaranteed minimum breaking load;

(*b*) its safe working load has been certificated by a competent person and in the case of a sling has been marked on in accordance with the requirements of paragraph 20.6.3;

(*c*) its diameter is more than 12 mm;

(*d*) it is made to a recognised national or international standard or to the requirements of a classification society; and

(*e*) it has been inspected in accordance with the requirements of Appendix subparagraph C.1.5(2).

10.1.2. (1) A rope composed of man-made fibre should not be used—

(*a*) if it has knots in it; or

(*b*) on a pulley block that does not meet the requirements of Chapter 12.

(2) A rope composed of man-made fibre should not be reeved through a pulley block on which the width of the groove of a sheave is less than the diameter of the rope or on which a sheave has any defect likely to cause damage to the rope.

10.1.3. A rope composed of man-made fibre should not be surged, paid out or rendered by slacking away the rope.[1]

10.2. Safe working load

10.2.1. The safe working load of a fibre rope should be determined by dividing its guaranteed minimum breaking load by a

---

1 Because these operations will give rise to frictional heat on a winch or capstan.

coefficient of utilisation determined in accordance with the requirements of Appendix section E.2.

10.3. Splices and other connections

10.3.1. (1) A rope composed of man-made fibre should not be—

(*a*) respliced if worn; or

(*b*) spliced to a natural fibre rope.

(2) When a rope composed of man-made fibre is joined to a wire rope, a thimble should be fitted to the eye of the fibre rope and the two ropes should have the same direction of lay.

10.3.2. (1) A thimble or loop splice in a rope should have—

(*a*) for polymide and polyester fibre rope, not less than four tucks each with all the yarns in the strands, followed by a further tuck with approximately half the material cut out of each strand, and a final tuck with not less than approximately a quarter of the original number of yarns; and

(*b*) for polypropylene fibre rope, not less than three full tucks, each with all the yarns in the strands.

(2) All tucks should be against the lay of the rope.

(3) Tails protruding from the rope should be of a length of not less than three rope diameters.

10.4. Endless slings

10.4.1. In the case of an endless sling, the requirements of section 10.3 should be complied with in respect of each side of the joining splice.

10.5. Care

10.5.1. (1) Ropes composed of man-made fibre should not be unduly exposed to sunlight, and when they are not in use they should be kept covered by tarpaulins or stowed below deck or in the store.

(2) Ropes composed of man-made fibre should not be allowed to come into contact with hot surfaces (such as steam pipes) or stored near radiated heat such as is given off by steam heaters.

10.5.2. Ropes composed of man-made fibre should be suitably protected by packing with rags, timber or other material when secured to any goods or cargo having sharp edges.

10.5.3. When subjected to a severe shock load or accidentally overloaded, a rope composed of man-made fibre should be taken out of service for up to 12 hours in order that it may recover its natural length (i.e. for the hysteresis effect to disappear).

10.5.4. If it is suspected that a rope composed of man-made fibre has come into contact with such organic solvents as paint stripper, paint or coal tar, it should be thoroughly washed as soon as possible and be inspected for damage.

11. Natural fibre rope

11.1. Fibre quality

11.1.1. Natural fibre rope for use on a lifting appliance or for slings should be of good grade manila (abaca) or other fibre of equal quality.

11.2. Compliance with other requirements

11.2.1. The rope should comply with the requirements of section 10.1 and paragraphs 10.2.1 and 10.5.2.

11.3. Thimble or loop splice

11.3.1. A thimble or loop splice in a rope should have not less than three full tucks, each tuck with all the yarns in the strand.

11.4. Care

11.4.1. When a rope is not in use, it should be stored in a suitable place, hung upon wooden pegs or galvanised hooks in a ventilated position away from any source of heat.

11.4.2. A rope that has become wet should be dried naturally.

11.4.3. A rope that has been or is suspected of having been in contact with any acid, alkali or any other substance known to be detrimental to fibre rope should be taken out of service and destroyed unless in the case of a long rope the area of contamination is definitely known, in which case that area may be cut out and respliced.

11.4.4. In some cases, it is advantageous to use only ropes that have been suitably treated with a rot-proofing agent and/or a water repellant.

11.4.5. A rope intended to be used for a boatswain's chair should be suitably tested before a person is hoisted in the chair.[1]

---

[1] One test is to use successive parts of the rope for a tug of war, with three men either side, the tension being applied progressively, i.e. first one man at each end of the rope, then two and finally three.

12. Pulley blocks for fibre ropes

12.1. General provisions

12.1.1. (1) A pulley block for use with rope consisting of man-made or natural fibre should have either a cast housing, or side and partition plates and straps of steel or of wood suitably reinforced with steel or aluminium straps.

(2) Except in the case of a cast housing, the side straps should be adequately and properly secured to the head fitting.

12.1.2. (1) The diameter of the sheave(s) measured at the bottom of the groove should not be less than 5.5 times the rope diameter it is designed for.

(2) The rope groove should have a depth of not less than a third of the diameter of the rope, the radius of the groove being not less than 1 mm greater than half the diameter of the rope.

12.1.3. As a general rule, the block should not be fitted with more than three sheaves and a becket, or four sheaves if the block is without a becket.

12.1.4. Provision should be made for the lubrication of all metal bearings and swivel head fittings and, where necessary, any plastic bearings.

12.2. Safe working load

12.2.1. The safe working load of the block should be assessed on the basis of use with best-grade manila rope.

12.3. Compliance with other requirements

12.3.1. The block should comply with the requirements of sub-paragraphs 4.2.1(*e*), 6.4.5(*d*), and 6.4.7(1) and (2), and as far as possible with section 6.5.

12.4. Block marking

12.4.1. The block should be marked with—

(*a*) the size of manila rope for which it has been designed;

(*b*) its own safe working load; and

(*c*) identification marks to relate it to its certificate of test and examination required under Appendix B, and where appropriate to the rigging plan.

13. Ship's cargo lifts[1]

13.1. Controls

13.1.1. A cargo lift should have controls that are—

(*a*) of the "dead man's" type;

(*b*) of the fail-safe type;

(*c*) so arranged, if fitted at each deck level, that only the controls on any one deck can be operated at a time; and

(*d*) so placed that—

(i) the operator is not in danger either from the lift or from vehicles or other moving objects on that deck; and

(ii) the operator is able to see the whole of the lift platform working surface at all times.

13.1.2. An independent emergency stop control should be fitted in a prominent position among or near the other controls.

13.2. Platform trip device

13.2.1. (1) A suitable trip device should be fitted beneath each side and end of the platform and beneath each side and end of each deck opening provided for the lift.

(2) When actuated, the trip device should be capable of promptly stopping movement of the platform so as to prevent as far as practicable any person, vehicle or cargo from being trapped.

13.3. Deck openings for cargo lift platforms

13.3.1. Each opening in a deck provided for a cargo lift platform should be protected by barriers that are—

(*a*) substantial and of a height of not less than 1 m above deck level

---

[1] See also section 4.2, which is applicable.

on each side of the opening that is not in use for vehicle access and egress;

(*b*) hinged or retractable on the side or sides of the opening in use;

(*c*) interlocked with the lift control so that the platform cannot be moved unless the barriers are all closed;

(*d*) so arranged that they cannot be opened unless the platform is at the opening controlled by them;

(*e*) situated as close to and above the edge of the opening as is practicable, in order that if any part of a vehicle or cargo carried should overlap the deck opening it will not be possible to close the barrier; and

(*f*) painted in alternate yellow and black warning stripes.

13.3.2. (1) A flashing warning light, preferably yellow, should be fitted on the deck side of each opening, at a place from which it can be readily seen from any vehicle on the deck.

(2) The light should operate continuously when the platform is away from the opening in that particular deck.

13.4. Slack rope device

13.4.1. Each suspension rope or chain of the lift should be fitted with a switch that will automatically cut off the power to the platform driving mechanism if for any reason a rope or chain becomes slack.

13.5. Locking latches

13.5.1. Where locking latches are fitted at any deck to enable the platform to be stowed during passage either with or without cargo on the platform, they should be interlocked in such a manner that—

(*a*) the power cannot be applied to the platform unless all the latches are withdrawn; and

(*b*) they cannot be withdrawn until the hydraulic system (when used) is pressurised sufficiently to support the lift.

13.6. Scissor lifts

13.6.1. A scissor lift should be provided with temporary fencing on any side of the lift from which it is not actually being loaded or unloaded at any time.

13.6.2. (1) The minimum clearance between the inside faces of any two outer arms should not be less than 3 cm.

(2) The minimum clearance between the inside face of any arm and the inside of the base frame structure should not be less than 5 cm.

13.6.3. The edges of the arms and frame structure referred to in paragraph 13.6.2. should be well radiused and smoothly finished.

13.6.4. No person other than the operator, the driver of a vehicle or persons loading or unloading the platform should be allowed near the lift when it is in use.

13.7 Carrying of passengers

13.7.1. No person should travel on a cargo lift platform; provided that this should not apply to the driver of a vehicle who remains at the controls of the vehicle.

13.8 Carrying of vehicles

13.8.1. A vehicle should have its brakes firmly applied whilst it is being carried on a lift.

14. Movement of vehicles on board ship

14.1. Vehicle movement control system

14.1.1. (1) A system of movement control of vehicles used in loading and unloading ships should be effectively and continuously applied.

(2) This plan should be prepared locally in full consultation with all concerned.

14.2. Loading and unloading ramps

14.2.1. (1) The slope of a ramp should not exceed one in ten.

(2) Where loading or unloading of the ship takes place in tidal waters, a suitable span link or floating bridge should be installed to ensure that the ramp slope will not exceed that angle.

14.2.2. In the case of a ramp capable of carrying only one vehicle at a time, precedence of movement on the ramp should be given to a loaded vehicle.

14.2.3. If a ramp is capable of dealing with simultaneous two-way traffic or there are two separate ramps in use, the direction of traffic should be clearly marked by arrows of sufficient size which should be illuminated when loading or unloading takes place at night or in poor light.

14.2.4. (1) The ramp should be protected to prevent a vehicle or a person from falling from its sides.

(2) A ship's ramp should fit into an area so protected.

14.3. Tractors

14.3.1. (1) Tractors used for towing trailers should—

(*a*) be suitable for the trailers; and

(*b*) have ample braking power to control a loaded trailer when using the loading ramp.

(2) Where there is any danger of rearing or broncoing, i.e. that the front of the tractor may rise suddenly on its rear wheels when the tractor accidentally jerks forward—

(*a*) the driving seat should be fitted with a lap and diagonal seat-belt, preferably of the inertia reel type; and

(*b*) the driver should always use the belt.

14.4. Signaller

14.4.1. When a large vehicle, trailer or heavy load on any special trailer of its own is being manœuvred into its stowing position on the deck, the driver should be under the direction of a signaller and—

(*a*) the driver should not move the load unless the signaller so directs;

(*b*) if at any time the signaller is not within the field of vision of the driver, the driver should immediately stop the vehicle;

(*c*) the signaller should wear an outer garment of a distinctive colour, preferably fluorescent yellow; and

(*d*) the signaller should satisfy himself that no person is in a position of danger, particularly in any trapping area, behind a reversing load.

14.5. Authorised persons

14.5.1. Only authorised persons should be allowed on any deck whilst loading or unloading of cargo by vehicles is taking place.

14.6. Enclosed decks

14.6.1. At every enclosed deck—

(*a*) effective steps should be taken to reduce the noise level from ventilating fans and other sources of noise to an acceptable minimum;

(*b*) adequate ventilation for the removal of fumes from vehicles using the deck should be provided;

(*c*) adequate lighting should be provided for every part of the deck;

(*d*) every fixed structure such as a stanchion column liable to be a danger to vehicles or to give rise to a trapping risk between a vehicle and the stanchion should be suitably marked in alternating black and yellow stripes; and

(*e*) whilst loading and unloading is taking place, the area should be kept clear, so far as is practicable, of dunnage, loose wires, vehicles, securing gear and other extraneous equipment or material.

15. Freight container terminals[1]

15.1. Definitions

15.1.1. For the purpose of this code—

(*a*) a "freight container terminal" is the whole area, which may be separate from or within a dock [1] complex, in which containerised cargo is handled;

(*b*) a "stacking area" is an area where freight containers are systematically stacked, one upon another, as necessary, in rows, awaiting onward movement either to a ship or to a road vehicle;

(*c*) a "block" is a sub-area of the stacking area separated by avenues from other blocks in the same stacking area; the block is divided into rows by aisles;

(*d*) an "aisle" is a passage, of sufficient width to enable a lifting appliance to pass along, between rows of freight containers;

(*e*) an "avenue" is a thoroughfare between blocks of containers, of a width amply sufficient to enable lifting appliances to manœuvre freely and to enter and leave aisles;

(*f*) a "straddle carrier" is a particular form of mobile lifting appliance in the form of a bridge having side supports on wheels of limited width such that the supports can move down adjacent aisles, the bridge straddling a row of stacked containers and being able to carry containers suspended beneath it;

(*g*) a "grid" is an area clearly designated and set aside for the loading and unloading of freight containers on to and from road transport vehicles by lifting appliances, particularly straddle carriers;

(*h*) a "slot" is a clearly marked out sub-area of a grid, just sufficient in size to accommodate one road vehicle of maximum size; and

(*i*) the "control centre" is the centre from which all operations in a terminal are centrally controlled.

---

[1] Chapter 2 is applicable to the dock area of a freight container terminal.

15.2. Segregation

15.2.1. Appropriate means should be taken to prevent the entry of unauthorised persons and vehicles into the terminal.

15.3. Vehicle and pedestrian movement control

15.3.1. (1) The entry of vehicles and persons and their movement about the terminal should be controlled so far as is possible.

(2) There should be well defined vehicle and pedestrian routes.

(3) Where practicable, the pedestrian routes should be fenced to prevent people from straying accidentally into dangerous areas.

15.3.2. Taxis and private cars should be required to keep to the vehicle routes, and should not be permitted to enter the dock side area where containers are being loaded or unloaded from a ship.

15.3.3. (1) Unless they are regular visitors and are known to be in possession of the terminal rules, all pedestrians and vehicle drivers should be given a copy of those rules.

(2) The master of a ship should likewise be given a copy of the rules as soon as possible after the ship berths.

15.3.4. If the size of the terminal justifies a terminal bus service for the conveyance of ships' visitors, ships' crews and other persons engaged in the operation of the terminal, such a service should be provided.

15.3.5. Vehicles from outside the terminal that may require to leave the vehicle route, such as vehicles carrying mooring crews or food and stores for ships, should be escorted by a terminal vehicle.

15.3.6. All terminal vehicles should be fitted with a flashing yellow warning light.

15.3.7. Where an authorised vehicle route must of necessity cross an avenue used by straddle carriers or other lifting appliances, signs and where necessary traffic lights should be provided giving precedence to the lifting appliances.

15.3.8. Where possible, grids should be designed to give one-way flow of traffic for the road vehicles conveying the containers. Vehicles should not reverse on to a grid unless there is ample space for this operation to be carried out in a safe manner.

15.3.9. The slots in the grid should be laid out in echelons or some other parallel fashion and, as a general rule, spaced not less than 3 m apart (6 m from centre to centre) if the grid is served by straddle carriers.

15.3.10. Vehicles used to transport containers should be so equipped as to ensure that containers are—

(*a*) supported by the corner fittings only or by the intermediate load transferring areas in the base structure; and

(*b*) attached to the vehicle by the twist hooks or equally acceptable means.

15.4. Control staff

15.4.1. The control staff should ensure that—

(*a*) any passengers carried in a visiting container vehicle descend from the vehicle before it is driven on to the grid and wait in a suitable waiting room provided for that purpose;

(*b*) the container-securing twist locks are released before the vehicle moves on to the grid, and that on departure the twist locks for the container loaded are not secured until after the vehicle is clear of the grid and in an area where it is safe to do so;

(*c*) during loading or unloading, the vehicle driver leaves the cab and stands at a safe distance from the vehicle (forward of the cab if the operation is carried out by straddle carrier) and does not return to the cab until the container loading appliance has departed from the grid;

(*d*) to load or unload a vehicle a straddle carrier approaches and leaves it via the rear;

(*e*) if an oversize container or problem container cannot be safely handled at the grid, it is removed to an area specially set apart for that purpose; and

(*f*) the grid is used solely for loading and unloading freight containers from road vehicles.

15.5. Row ends

15.5.1. The ends of rows should, where practicable, be stepped down in order to improve the visibility of straddle carriers emerging from the stack.

15.6. Wind

15.6.1. Where experience has shown that the wind force, whether continued or in gusts, is apt to displace a container stacked upon another container or containers, no person should be permitted to enter the area on foot after a warning has been received that the wind speed has reached a predetermined level.

15.7. Permit to enter

15.7.1. In the case of a stack served by straddle carriers or where the visibility of the lifting appliance is limited owing to the closeness of the rows of containers and their stacking height, no persons should be permitted to enter the stack unless they have been issued by the control centre with permits to enter.

15.7.2. Subject to the remaining provisions of this section, a permit to enter should be designed to suit the particular terminal and the local conditions.

15.7.3. (1) The permit to enter should be issued by the control centre.

(2) The block control officer should notify the drivers of the straddle carriers or other lifting appliances he controls of the block that is to be isolated for the entry of a person.

(3) When each driver has acknowledged the message, the officer in charge of the control centre should pass the permit to the block control officer.

(4) The permit should not be issued until the control centre is satisfied that—

(*a*) the person who is to enter the block is wearing a high-visibility outer garment of the correct colour (different colours for different duties are permitted);

(*b*) the person has been issued with a two-way radio and is familiar with its use;

(*c*) the necessary particulars, including the person's name, the duty to be performed and the time of entry, have been entered on the permit;

(*d*) where there is more than one person, the leader of the party has been made responsible for the party and has been issued with the two-way radio; and

(*e*) the person has been instructed not to leave the block until the control centre has been notified of this intention by radio and consent has been received.

15.7.4. (1) The block isolated for a person's entry should be clearly flagged on the stacking area plan in control.

(2) Each straddle carrier should have a board in the cab upon which the driver enters an indication of the block that has been isolated.

15.7.5. (1) The control officer and the driver of the carrier should inform the relief driver of the position of the isolated block upon change of shift.

(2) The permit should not be transferred.

15.7.6. The block control officer should check the return of the permit for cancellation; if it has not been returned after a reasonable time, he should take suitable steps to ascertain why, and if necessary the whereabouts of the missing person.

15.8. Unauthorised persons in stacking area

15.8.1. Should a carrier driver see a stranger, i.e. a person not wearing the coloured garment referred to in subparagraph 15.7.3(4)(*a*), in the stacking area, the driver should immediately inform the control centre, which in turn should order the movement of all carriers in the stacking area to cease forthwith until the stranger has been located and brought out of the stacking area.

15.9. Emergency signals

15.9.1. In an emergency such as an accident or fire, the control centre should send by radio a clear instruction or signal of such a nature that is immediately recognised as an emergency signal, whereupon all movement of vehicles should cease immediately in order to give free passage with the minimum of danger to ambulances, fire brigades, and other rescue personnel and equipment.

15.10. Unserviceable, damaged or unsafe equipment

15.10.1. Unserviceable vehicles, plant, containers and other equipment should be removed from the operation area and be clearly and suitably marked to ensure that they are not used until they have been repaired.

15.10.2. (1) All outbound containers arriving at a terminal should be inspected for damage affecting safe handling, and appropriate measures should be taken if the containers are found to be unsafe to handle.

(2) Damaged containers arriving in a vessel should be handled by such special means as will ensure safety.

15.10.3. The actual weight of all loaded containers should be ascertained before hoisting. Containers exceeding the maximum allowable weight or the capacity of the handling equipment should not be handled.

15.10.4. (1) Shippers should be advised as to the proper stowage of cargo in containers, particularly as to weight distribution and weight limitations.

(2) Weight distribution should as far as possible be uniform throughout the floor area of containers.

15.11. Hazardous cargo

15.11.1. Containers containing dangerous or hazardous contents should be stacked in an area set apart from the main stack and be clearly labelled and railed off, or be otherwise stored in a safe manner in accordance with national regulations or international regulations such as those of the Inter-Governmental Maritime Consultative Organisation (IMCO).

15.12. Customs inspections

15.12.1. (1) Safe areas with safe means of access should be provided for containers required to be examined by customs officers.

(2) Where customs officers need to go into the stacks, they should comply with the permit-to-enter system.

15.13. Hoisting of intermodal freight containers

15.13.1. (1) Intermodal freight containers, when hoisted from the top corner fittings, should, if 6 m or more in length, be hoisted only by a vertical lift from all four fittings.

(2) Slings attached to those fittings at an angle from the vertical should not be used.

(3) When a container is lifted by the four bottom corner fittings, angled slings may be used; provided that their angle and attachment correspond to those intended in the design of the container.

(4) In all cases, the means of attachment of lifting devices to the container corners should be suitable for the purpose.

15.14. Terminal equipment

15.14.1. The entry of road vehicles to the grid slots should be controlled so that only one vehicle is in a slot at the same time.

15.14.2. Skeletal vehicles should be fitted on each side, between the outer extremities of the front and rear transverse beams, with longitudinal bars, taut wires or chains.

15.14.3. Each area set aside for maintenance of vehicles or equipment should be clearly marked.

16. Access to the top of a container

16.1. Examination area

16.1.1. Any freight container requiring detailed examination should be removed from the stack and placed in an area which is specially set apart for this purpose and in which safe means of access such as aircraft-type steps, fixed access platforms or ladders may be provided.

16.2. Means of access

16.2.1. (1) In the case of a stack, special equipment such as the type of access platform fitted to articulated arms mounted on a road vehicle for the maintenance of street lights should be employed whenever this is practicable.

(2) Alternatively, a straddle carrier may be employed, after it has been specially adapted for this use, to enable a person to travel on the carrier and, when the latter is positioned over the particular container, to be able to pass on to the container in safety, the carrier remaining stationary the whole time.

(3) The modification referred to in subparagraph (2) should not be such as to impair the suitability of the straddle carrier for the work for which it was originally designed.

(4) A suitable standard operating procedure for the transport of persons should be laid down to suit the type of carrier and local conditions.

(5) This procedure should include a strict requirement that the driver of the carrier shall—

(*a*) obey all instructions from the person examining the container when that person is descending on to or climbing from or standing on the container;

(*b*) not move any part of the carrier's mechanism when the other person is not within his field of vision; and (*c*) ignore audible instructions from the other person, which should be prohibited.

16.2.2. (1) In the case of a ship which is purpose-built to carry containers stacked upon its deck, safe means of access should form a permanent part of the ship's equipment.

(2) This means of access should consist of a stowable gantry frame running on rails, capable of spanning a container or containers, and provided in particular with suitable ladders and guarded walkways together with means for locking the gantry against movement at any position on the deck, or any other arrangement or apparatus giving like safety.

16.2.3. (1) Where a ship is not provided with a safe means of access as required under paragraph 16.2.2, the main lifting frame of the dockside crane, suitably adapted without prejudice to its normal use, should be used, or a separate safety frame.

(2) The signaller, or when practicable any person ascending on to the container, should be in radio, visual or telephone communication with the crane driver, and the latter should obey instructions only from that person.

16.2.4. A person gaining access to the top of a container by the foregoing means should be suitably protected against the danger of falling where appropriate by wearing a suitable safety harness properly tethered, or by other effective means, whilst on the container.

17. Vacuum lifting devices[1]

17.1. Measuring, warning and pressure-reducing equipment

17.1.1. (1) Every vacuum lifting device should be fitted with a suitable vacuum gauge or other device that—

(*a*) gives the driver of the lifting appliance of which it forms a part a visual indication of the state of the vacuum at any time;

(*b*) is of sufficient size and located in a position such that the gauge reading may be easily read at the attachment and release positions of the load; and

(*c*) is distinctively marked with a red mark to indicate the lowest vacuum below which the appliance should not be used.

(2) Every vacuum lifting device should be fitted with a device that gives an audible warning to the driver and any person working in the vicinity at ground level when the vacuum is 80 per cent or less of the designed working vacuum, and/or if the vacuum-inducing pump ceases to operate.

(3) Every vacuum lifting device should be fitted with means which, in the event of failure of the vacuum-inducing pump, will maintain sufficient vacuum to continue to support the load suspended for a sufficient time, including a safety margin, for that load to be safely deposited from the maximum height of lift of the lifting appliance to the level of the dock side.

17.2. Vacuum hoses

17.2.1. Every vacuum hose should be of a type suitable for the purpose.

17.3. Use

17.3.1. A vacuum device should be used only on cargo that is

[1] See also section 4.2 and Chapters 9 and 20, which are applicable.

specially wrapped for the purpose or has an otherwise suitable surface for vacuum lifting pads.

17.3.2. The vacuum device should be used in such a manner that—

(*a*) each pad supports so far as is practicable an equal part of the load;

(*b*) the load is suspended horizontally as far as this is possible;

(*c*) the surface of the cargo to be handled is clear of any loose material that would prevent any vacuum pad from making effective contact with the surface.

17.3.3. Vacuum lifting devices should not be used in any manner to transport persons.

17.4. Inspection

17.4.1. The vacuum device as a whole should be—

(*a*) thoroughly examined in accordance with the requirements of Appendix paragraph C.1.2; and

(*b*) inspected, particularly the hoses and vacuum pads, before use at the beginning of every shift or day, and the warning devices tested at the beginning of each week.

17.4.2. (1) The vacuum device should be tested by a competent person before being taken into use for the first time or after any substantial repair by raising a test load in accordance with the relevant requirements of subparagraph 4.2.1(*e*) and Appendix paragraph D.3.1.

(2) The test load surface should, so far as is practicable, be similar to the worst type of surface the device is intended to be used on, and in the case of wrapped cargo such as paper the test load should be similarly wrapped.

17.5. Controls

17.5.1. Where the vacuum is controlled from the cab of the lifting appliance supporting the device, the controls should be of a design that will prevent accidental removal of the vacuum.

17.5.2. The device should be marked in accordance with the requirements of section 20.6.

17.6. Designed working vacuum

17.6.1. The designed working vacuum of the device should be the vacuum necessary to support the test load required to be imposed by subparagraph 17.4.2(1).

17.7. Access to ship's hold

17.7.1. No person should be permitted in the hold of the ship or, in the case of a ship with 'tween decks, beneath the square of the hatch or in any other place where such a person would be liable to be struck by the load or by any part of the load falling from the device.

18. Magnetic lifting devices[1]

18.1. Electrical

18.1.1. The voltage of the electric supply to any magnetic lifting device should not fluctuate by more than ± 10 per cent.

18.1.2. (1) A magnetic lifting device should be provided with an alternative supply of power, i.e. batteries that come into operation immediately in the event of failure of the main power; provided that this subparagraph need not apply to a magnet that is being used to load or unload scrap metal or to other cargo-handling operations of such a nature that there is no person in the vicinity other than the driver of the lifting appliance.

(2) A magnetic lifting device should be so constructed as to withstand the entry of moisture.

18.2. Inspection

18.2.1. A magnetic lifting device should be thoroughly examined in accordance with the requirements of Appendix paragraph C.1.2.

18.3. Safe working load

18.3.1. (1) A magnetic lifting device should be marked with its safe working load as determined by tests using weights of the same characteristics as the load for which the device is intended to be used.

(2) When the load to be lifted is dissimilar to the test load, it should be restricted to approximately 60 per cent of the safe working load.

18.4. Precautions when in use

18.4.1. (1) The power to the magnet should not be switched on until after the magnet has been lowered on to the load to be lifted.

---

[1] See also sections 4.2, 17.7 and 20.6, which are applicable.

(2) After the power has been switched on, the lifting motion should be delayed for a few seconds (up to ten seconds in the case of scrap metal).

(3) The device should be carefully lowered on to the load, and not dropped.

(4) It should not be allowed to strike a solid obstacle while the lifting appliance is being operated.

(5) It should not be used to lift a steel sheet from a pile of sheets unless care is taken to ensure that sheets beneath the sheet to be lifted are detached.

(6) The device should not be used on hot metal.

(7) When not in use, the power should be switched off to prevent the magnets from becoming too hot.

(8) When not in use, the device should not remain deposited on the ground but be supported by suitable means intended for the purpose.

(9) Magnetic lifting devices should not be used to transport persons.

19. Fork-lift trucks[1]

19.1. General provisions

19.1.1. When it is necessary for drivers to leave fork-lift trucks or tractors unattended, the engines should be stopped, the brakes applied, the operating controls locked, the forks tilted forward flush with the floor and clear of the passageway and, if the vehicle is on a dangerous incline, the wheels blocked.

19.1.2. Workers should not jump on or off moving vehicles.

19.2. Driver protection

19.2.1. (1) The truck should be fitted with an overhead guard of sufficient strength to protect the driver so far as is practicable against the impact of small objects falling from above.

(2) The manufacturer should certify that the prototype of the guard has been tested both statically and dynamically in accordance with a national and international standard.

19.2.2. A suitable back rest should be attached to the fork carrier in order so far as is practicable to prevent objects carried on the forks from falling on to the driver.

19.3. Hydraulic system

19.3.1. Flexible hoses, piping, unions and connections should be of adequate strength (generally capable of withstanding a pressure of three times the maximum working pressure without bursting).

19.3.2. A restrictor device should be fitted capable of restricting the speed of descent of the load carriage to not more than 0.6 m/s in the event of a failure in the system such as a pipe burst.

19.3.3. If a relief valve is provided, it should either be non-

[1] See also section 4.2, which is applicable.

adjustable or if adjustable be suitably locked against unauthorised interference.

19.4. Travel-limiting devices

19.4.1. Devices should be fitted to limit automatically the extent of upward movement of the forks, and also of downward movement unless the lowering motion is non-powered.

19.5. Forks

19.5.1. The forks should be designed to prevent their accidental unhooking or lateral displacement when in use.

19.5.2. The forks of a truck should be separately tested by a competent person in accordance with a national or international standard before being taken into use.

19.5.3. Fork attachments such as rotating heads and drum or bale clamps should be used whenever their use would be justified by the volume of cargo handled.

19.5.4. Any trapping points between the fork arm mechanism and any fixed parts of the truck should be suitably guarded.

19.6. Slinging points

19.6.1. Any trucks, and any battery containers in the case of electric trucks, that are intended to be hoisted aboard ship should have suitable slinging points.

19.7. Steering

19.7.1. In the case of a truck fitted with non-powered steering, the steering wheel should be designed to prevent, so far as is practicable, the driver's hands from being injured if one of the truck wheels strikes a kerb or other fixed object or dunnage in the road.

19.8. Tyre pressure

19.8.1. The tyre pressures should be conspicuously marked on the chassis next to the respective wheels.

19.9. Stability testing

19.9.1. Every prototype or modified truck should be stability-tested by a competent person in accordance with a national or international standard before it is taken into use.

19.10. Safe operation of trucks

19.10.1. (1) Before drivers begin to use a truck, they should satisfy themselves that it is in safe condition.

(2) Any defects should be reported to the supervisor.

19.10.2. Tyre pressures should be checked daily.

19.10.3. A truck should not be used to handle a load greater than its capacity marked upon it.[1]

19.10.4. Passengers should not be carried, particularly on the forks.

19.10.5. (1) The forks should be adjusted to their correct width.

(2) The forks should be placed fully under the load, which should be equally distributed, so far as is practicable, between the forks.

19.10.6. No load should be carried or raised with the mast tilting forward.

19.10.7. When travelling, the fork arms should be lowered to their lowest practicable position, in general not more than 15 cm above the ground.

19.10.8. When the load obscures the driver's forward vision, the truck should be driven in reverse.

---

[1] See paragraph 19.14.2, which is applicable.

19.10.9. (1) When a truck is being driven on an incline, the load should always face up the slope.

(2) When a truck is being driven without any load, the forks should face down the slope.

19.10.10. (1) Special care should be taken when driving a truck—

(*a*) if the ground is slippery;

(*b*) to avoid any loose dunnage or waste;

(*c*) when passing by or through doorways used by personnel;

(*d*) when rounding a corner where vision is restricted;

(*e*) in any place where the overhead clearance is limited;

(*f*) near any open hatch or lift opening on a ship when the lift platform is away from that deck;

(*g*) on bridges over trenches or other gaps.

(2) When a truck is travelling on the platform of a ship's lift, special care should be taken to ensure that—

(*a*) the truck is so placed that no part of it or of the load projects beyond the edge of the platform;

(*b*) the truck brakes are firmly applied; and

(*c*) the driver stays at the controls of the truck.

19.10.11. No person should be allowed to stand or pass under the elevated forks.

19.10.12. (1) When the truck is stacking goods, the stack should be approached slowly with the mast still tilted backwards.

(2) When the truck is sufficiently close to and facing the stack, the forks should be raised until they are slightly above the stacking level, the brakes of the truck having been applied.

(3) When the load is over the stack, the mast should be brought to its vertical position and the load deposited.

(4) Once the load is properly stacked, the forks should be with-

drawn from beneath the load (with the mast tilting forward if necessary by backing the truck away from the stack).

(5) The forks should then be lowered to the travelling position.

19.10.13. (1) When the truck is unstacking goods, it should approach the stack and stop with the forks approximately 30 cm from the stack face.

(2) The driver should check that the forks are at the correct width and the load within the capacity of the truck.

(3) With forks raised to the correct height and the mast tilted forward, the truck should be moved forward until the forks are completely beneath the load, and the brakes of the truck should then be applied.

(4) The forks should be raised until the load is just clear of the stack and the mast should be tilted slightly backwards. Great care should be taken that any other load on the stack is not disturbed during this operation.

(5) The driver should ensure that the way is clear, and should reverse the truck sufficiently far from the stack to clear the road.

(6) The load should then be lowered to the travelling position, the mast should be tilted fully backwards and the truck should then move off steadily.

19.10.14. Fork arms should be fully lowered when the truck is parked.

19.10.15. No attempt should be made to handle a heavy load by the simultaneous use of two trucks.

19.10.16. Another vehicle should not be towed or pushed by a fork-lift truck unless it has proper attachments fitted for that purpose.

19.10.17. The truck should not pick up, put down or carry a load on a slope that runs across the fore-and-aft centre line of the truck.

19.10.18. (1) Unsafe loads should not be carried.

(2) The load should be secure and safely bonded, and pallets should not be overfilled.

19.10.19. Where material handling vehicles are used in a 'tween deck and the coaming is raised, appropriate means of bridging should be provided and it should be adequately secured.

19.11. Pedestrian-controlled pallet trucks

19.11.1. A pedestrian-controlled pallet truck should comply with the relevant provisions of Chapter 4.

19.11.2. The maximum speed for the truck should at all times be limited by the local conditions, and should in no case exceed 6 km/h.

19.11.3. The operator should always walk with the truck and not attempt to ride upon it.

19.11.4. When it is necessary for the driver to precede the truck, he should walk to one side of the control handle and clear of the truck.

19.11.5. When approaching an obstacle, the driver should, whenever possible, be behind the truck.

19.11.6. When the truck is used for loading or unloading a large vehicle by driving upon it, a check should be made to ensure that—

(*a*) the large vehicle's brakes are firmly applied;

(*b*) the bridge spanning the gap between the loading platform or bay and the large vehicle is sound, of adequate strength and firmly positioned; and

(*c*) the vehicle's loading surface is strong enough and in good and level condition.

19.11.7. When a truck is required to use a goods lift, the driver should—

(*a*) approach the lift, load first;

(*b*) stop at a safe distance from the gate;

(*c*) check that the combined weight of the truck and its load is within the safe working load of the lift;

(*d*) check that the floor of the lift is level with the ground or loading floor, as the case may be;

(*e*) check that the load will clear the lift entrance;

(*f*) drive on very slowly and with great caution; and

(*g*) firmly apply the brakes and shut off the power.

19.12. Reach and straddle trucks

19.12.1. A truck should not be driven with its reach mechanism extended.

19.12.2. Before the reach mechanism is operated, the brakes of the truck should be properly applied.

19.12.3. No person should be allowed to step over the reach legs while the truck is in use.

19.12.4. A check should be made to ensure that the load is raised above the reach legs before they are retracted.

19.13. Side-loading fork-lift trucks

19.13.1. The load should be raised clear of the deck before traversing in.

19.13.2. (1) If stabilising jacks are fitted, they should be firmly applied before lifting the load.

(2) If stabilising jacks are not fitted, the load should not exceed the derated load appropriate to operating without the stabilising jacks applied.

19.13.3. Before travel takes place, the load should be firmly on the deck and the forks just clear underneath, unless a backward tilt is used to stabilise a loose load.

19.13.4. The truck should not move while the mast is in the traversed-out position.

19.13.5. When a side-loading fork-lift truck is used for stacking, the procedure to be followed is as given below—

(*a*) the stack should be approached with the load placed on the deck of the truck, utilising backward deck tilt (if fitted);

(*b*) the truck should stop when the load is in line with the depositing position and the truck is parallel to the stack;

(*c*) the stabilising jacks, if any, should be firmly applied;

(*d*) any deck tilt should be removed;

(*e*) the load should be raised to the required height;

(*f*) the load should be traversed out until over the stacking position;

(*g*) the load should be lowered on to the stack, any tilt being corrected as necessary;

(*h*) when the load is properly stacked, the forks should be lowered until free of the pallet or dunnage strips;

(*i*) the mast should be traversed fully in and the forks lowered to just below deck level; and

(*j*) the stabilising jacks, if any, should then be retracted or raised.

19.13.6. The procedure for destacking is the reverse of the procedure for stacking.

19.14. General precautions

19.14.1. A special attachment consisting of a frame fitted to the fork-anchoring frame and fitted with a conventional hook should be used only if—

(*a*) its safe working load, including that for traversing on a slope, has been assessed by the maker of the truck or a competent person and is marked upon it;

(*b*) the maximum height of lift of the hook is conspicuously marked upon the mast of the truck;

(*c*) the attachment has been properly tested and the hook complies with the requirements of section 20.10; and (*d*) proper steps are taken to ensure that swing of the suspended load is controlled when the truck is traversing.

19.14.2. (1) The safe working load or loads (where there is more than one load owing to the use of such devices as stabilisers or extension forks) should be marked upon a truck.

(2) The weight of the truck should be marked upon it.

(3) In the case of electric trucks—

(*a*) the marking required under subparagraph (2) should include the weight both with and without the battery and battery container; and

(*b*) the battery container should be marked with the combined total weight of the container and the battery.

19.14.3. Tyres should be frequently checked for damage, particularly the tyre walls.

19.14.4. No counterweight should be added to increase the lifting capacity.

19.14.5. The truck should be driven cautiously and its audible warning device (horn or klaxon) sounded as necessary when—

(*a*) pedestrians are in the vicinity;

(*b*) passing through rubber swing doors;

(*c*) passing any concealed entrances, parked vehicles or large obstacles such as temporarily stowed crates.

19.14.6. When a tractor truck is towing other trailer trucks—

(*a*) corner cutting or taking a corner too sharply should be avoided;

(*b*) if a wide load is being towed, plenty of clearance should be allowed when passing other trucks, stationary objects or people at work;

(*c*) when reversing, assistance should be sought if necessary;

(*d*) as a general rule, reversing should not take place if there is more than one trailer;

(*e*) the truck should be driven slowly down gradients when the trailers are loaded, particularly if the trailers are not fitted with overrun brakes; and

(*f*) brakes should not be applied too fiercely.[1]

19.15. Equipment

19.15.1. All truck and tractor equipment should be of good material, of sound construction, sufficiently strong for the purposes for which it is used, and kept in a good state of repair.

19.15.2. Tractors, power trucks and hand trucks should where practicable be equipped with rubber tyres and with ball-bearings or roller bearings.

19.15.3. When not in use, trucks and tractors should be kept in regular storage places and protected from the weather.

19.15.4. All truck and tractor equipment should be inspected at least once a week by maintenance men or other competent persons, and when any dangerous defect is discovered in a vehicle it should be immediately taken out of service.

19.16. Lights

19.16.1. Where power trucks or tractors are used in inadequately lighted places, they should be provided with headlights and tail lamps.

19.17. Seats

19.17.1. The seats on power trucks and tractors should be properly sprung to prevent excessive jolting of the drivers.

19.18. Platforms

19.18.1. The operating platforms of power trucks and tractors should be provided with substantial guards to prevent the operators

---

[1] Because this may cause the trailers to jack-knife.

from being crushed in the event of collision with other trucks or with obstacles.

19.19. Electric trucks

19.19.1. (1) An electrically driven truck or tractor should be fitted with at least one adequate mechanical brake and a mechanically operated current cut-off that comes into operation automatically when the operator leaves the vehicle.

(2) When the vehicle is stationary, it should not be possible to close the circuit unless the operative parts of the switch apparatus (controller) have passed through neutral.

19.19.2. Measures should be taken to prevent spillage of the electrolyte used in electric battery trucks, for instance by using the minimum necessary quantity of distilled water, or bedding the batteries on to shock absorbers and providing drip trays.

19.20. Hand trucks

19.20.1. Hand trucks used for transporting carboys or similar objects should be designed and constructed for that specific purpose.

19.20.2. If hand trucks are used on inclined surfaces, or if it is advisable to prevent them from moving when left standing, they should be provided with effective brakes.

19.20.3. Three-wheeled or four-wheeled hand trucks should be provided with spring clips or other locking devices by which the handles can be secured in an upright position, and which the truckers should be required to use when the trucks are standing still.

19.20.4. Handles of hand trucks should be so designed as to protect the hands, or be provided with knuckle-guards.

19.21. Batteries

19.21.1. The batteries of a truck should be handled, whether for charging, removal or other purposes, only in a proper place especially set aside for that purpose and under the supervision of an experienced person.

19.22. Refuelling of petrol trucks

19.22.1. When a petrol truck is refuelled—

(*a*) the engine should be stopped and the operator off the truck during refuelling;

(*b*) where possible, a truck should be refuelled from a conventional pump at a properly equipped garage;

(*c*) refuelling from containers should preferably be carried out in the open, or at any rate only in a well ventilated space, and well clear of stored goods, inflammable material or a naked light; no petrol truck should be refuelled in a confined space, including a hold or other compartment;

(*d*) care should be taken to prevent spillage or overfilling of the truck's tank;

(*e*) the filler cap should be properly replaced, and any spilled fuel disposed of by sponging with non-combustible absorbent material before the engine is restarted;

(*f*) smoking should be prohibited;

(*g*) any bare, heated engine surfaces likely to ignite spilled fuel should be properly protected.

19.23. Refuelling of trucks with liquefied petroleum gas (LPG)

19.23.1. Containers of liquefied petroleum gas should be changed only by a fully trained person assigned to such duties.

19.23.2. (1) Whenever possible, the exchange or removal of containers should be carried out in the open.

(2) When this operation is carried out indoors or on a ship's deck, the truck should be fitted with means of reducing to a minimum the escape of fuel when the containers are exchanged (for example,

an automatic quick-closing coupling in the fuel line, or a valve, the engine being allowed to run until the fuel in the line has been consumed).

19.23.3. Particular care should be taken to ensure that the thread on the truck's feed union is in perfect condition and is gas-tight when properly screwed up.

19.23.4. The container should be installed with its safety valve on top, so as to ensure that the container's valve aperture leads into its vapour space.

19.23.5. Fuel containers should be handled with extreme care at all times, and be stored in a suitable place away from any source of heat and with their safety valves uppermost.

19.23.6. Every fuel container should be free from dents, scrapes, gouges or other similar defects, and all fittings should be in good working order.

19.23.7. No smoking should be allowed in any area where containers are stored or in the container changing area.

19.24. Vehicle exhaust emissions

19.24.1. Every internal combustion vehicle should be fitted with a suitable exhaust emission purifier and spark arrestor.

19.24.2. The vehicle exhaust system should be in good order, with no leaks and every join tightened so that it is gas-tight.

19.24.3. No truck powered by an internal combustion engine should be used in any enclosed space such as a ship's 'tween deck or a warehouse, unless that space, if it does not have sufficient natural ventilation, is provided with effective and adequate forced exhaust or supply ventilation with an intake of clean outside air for the removal of the products of combustion.

20. Loose gear

20.1. Definitions

20.1.1. For the purpose of this code, "loose gear" is defined as a hook, ring, shackle, link, lifting beam, lifting frame or any similar article of equipment by means of which a load may be attached to a lifting appliance and which does not form an integral part of the lifting appliance.

20.2. General provisions

20.2.1. Every item of loose gear should—

(*a*) be of good design and construction, of adequate strength for the purpose for which it is used, and free from any patent defect;

(*b*) be made to a recognised national or international standard;

(*c*) before being taken into use for the first time or after any repair or alteration to a stress-bearing part, be tested and certificated in accordance with the requirements of Appendix C by a competent person;

(*d*) be periodically thoroughly examined and inspected in accordance with the requirements of Appendix C by a competent person;

(*e*) be marked in accordance with the requirements of section 20.6; and

(*f*) be properly maintained in good order.

20.3. Use of wrought iron

20.3.1. (1) Wrought iron should not be used in the manufacture of any loose gear taken into use for the first time or in any subsequent repair of that gear.

(2) Any gear made wholly or in part of wrought iron should be scrapped as soon as is reasonably practicable.

(3) Until gear made wholly or in part of wrought iron is scrapped,

it should be periodically heat-treated in accordance with the requirements of Appendix G.

20.4. Heat treatment

20.4.1. Except as provided under subparagraph 20.3.1(3) and section 20.9, loose gear made of iron or steel should not be subjected to any form of heat treatment except—

(*a*) under the supervision of a competent person; and

(*b*) in an enclosed furnace (muffle) of a construction that ensures that the gear is heated uniformly, does not impart any gaseous impurity into the gear and is under accurate temperature control.

20.5. Steel

20.5.1. Every steel part of loose gear (other than wire rope) should be made of the same quality grade of steel.

20.6. Markings

20.6.1. (1) Every item of loose gear should be marked in a conspicuous place with its safe working load, means of identification, its own weight in the case of a lifting beam, lifting frame or similar gear, and, where appropriate, a mark to indicate the quality grade of the steel.

(2) The marking should be made on the article in a place where it will not give rise to stress.

(3) Where the marking is stamped directly on the gear, the stamps should not exceed the following sizes:

Safe working load—

up to and including 2 tonnes	3 mm
over 2 tonnes and up to and including 8 tonnes	4.5 mm
over 8 tonnes	6 mm

(4) Where the marking is stamped on the link of a chain or other part of gear having a circular section, the stamps should not exceed the following sizes:

Circular section—

up to and including 12.5 mm diameter	3 mm
over 12.5 mm and up to and including 26 mm	4.5 mm
over 26 mm	6 mm

(5) The stamp should give a concave indentation without sharp corners on the indentations and should not be struck with a blow greater than that necessary to result in a clear indentation.

(6) If the material is too hard or if direct marking would affect or be liable to affect the subsequent safe use of the gear, the marking should be carried out on some other suitable support such as a tablet, disc or ferrule, of durable material permanently attached to the gear, and in this case the size of the marking may be greater than the sizes indicated in subparagraphs (3) and (4), according to the discretion of the maker or other competent person.

20.6.2. The marking of the safe working load of a lifting beam, lifting frame and comparable gear should be made in a conspicuous position and should be of such a size as to be immediately legible to the person or persons using the gear.

20.6.3. The safe working load should be marked in any permanent manner such as—

(*a*) in the case of a sling having a terminal ring or link, on that ring or link;

(*b*) in the case of any other sling, on a tablet, disc or ferrule attached to the sling, provided that the attachment of the tablet, disc or ferrule to a wire or fibre rope should be such as not to cause damage to the rope;

(*c*) in the case of a wire rope having ferrule-secured eyes made in accordance with the requirements of paragraph 9.5.3, on a ferrule, provided that the marking is in conformity with the requirements of subparagraphs 20.6.1(3) and (4); and

(*d*) in the case of a webbed sling, on the sling itself.

20.6.4. The safe working load marked upon a multi-legged sling should be—

(*a*) in the case of a two-legged sling, the safe working load of the sling when the included angle between the legs is 90°;

(*b*) in the case of a three-legged sling, the safe working of the sling when the included angle between any two adjacent legs is 90°; and

(*c*) in the case of a four-legged sling, the safe working load of the sling when the included angle between any two diagonally opposite legs is 90°.

20.6.5. The quality grade mark placed on the steel should be in accordance with the requirements of Appendix F.

20.6.6. The safe working load of loose gear should be marked in accordance with the requirements of paragraph 4.13.4.

20.7. Construction of slings

20.7.1. Every wire or fibre rope used in the construction of a sling should comply with the requirements of Chapters 9, 10 and 11 so far as is appropriate.

20.8. Testing

20.8.1. No loose gear, other than wire rope, fibre rope or webbed sling material, should fail to the extent that it is no longer capable of sustaining a load at less than twice the proof test load applied to it in accordance with the requirements of Appendix D.

20.9. Welding

20.9.1. Where welding is carried out in the manufacture or repair of any loose gear—

(*a*) it should be carried out only by qualified workers using appropriate techniques; and

(*b*) where necessary and according to the instructions of the competent person responsible for certificating the gear in accordance with the requirements of Appendix C, the gear should be subjected to an appropriate heat treatment to restore the mechanical properties of the material or to relieve any stress in the material, or for both purposes.

20.10. Hooks

20.10.1. Every hook should be—

(*a*) provided with an efficient device to prevent the displacement of the sling or load from the hook; or

(*b*) of such construction or shape as to prevent displacement.

20.10.2. (1) The screwed shank of a hook or any other similar thread should, at the point where the screwed portion terminates, be properly undercut to an extent not greater than the depth of the thread.

(2) If any plain portion of the shank terminates at a shoulder or flange of greater diameter, the corner so formed should be radiused as much as is practicable.

21. Use of loose gear

21.1. Safe working load

21.1.1. No loose gear should be subjected to a load greater than the safe working load marked upon it, except for the purpose of a proof test in accordance with the requirements of subparagraph 4.2.1(*e*).

21.2. Multi-legged sling

21.2.1. No multi-legged sling should be used—

(*a*) with any of its legs at an angle greater than the included angle indicated in paragraph 20.6.4.; or

(*b*) with a load greater than the safe working load marked upon it when the included angle is less than that indicated in paragraph 20.6.4.

21.3. Storage

21.3.1. When not in use, loose gear such as chains, wire rope and fibre rope should be stored under cover in clean, dry, well ventilated places where it is free from excessive heat and protected against corrosion.

21.3.2. Loose gear in storage should be raised from the ground, and not be in contact with damaging agents such as ashes, clinker or coke breeze.

21.3.3. Storage arrangements for loose gear should not be such as to expose workers to risks from such factors as over-exertion or falling objects.

21.3.4. As far as is practicable, loose gear in storage should be so arranged that chains, wire ropes and fibre ropes with the same safe working load are grouped together, the fibre ropes being separated from the metal gear.

21.3.5. (1) Gear awaiting repair should be separately and suitably stored.

(2) Gear taken out of service and beyond repair should be scrapped.

21.4. Withdrawal from service

21.4.1. Loose gear should be withdrawn from service—

(*a*) if it has been overloaded or been subject to faulty heat treatment;

(*b*) if any part of it is worn by 8 per cent or more as a result of fair wear;

(*c*) if it is distorted, stretched or has any serious gouge or similar defects or any signs of cracks, particularly in the region of welds or at corners or changes of section;

(*d*) in the case of wire rope, if as described in subparagraph 9.9.1(*d*) to (*f*) it has any projecting broken wires or any broken wires in a splice or adjacent to a ferrule-secured eye fitting;

(*e*) in the case of fibre rope or webbed slings, if the rope has been in contact with any acid, alkali or other substance inimical to the fibres, yarns or material or if it has been seriously stretched, or has cuts, fraying or loosening of any splices; or

(*f*) if it has not been inspected in accordance with subparagraph 20.2.1(*d*).

21.5. Precautions during use

21.5.1. Loose gear should not be—

(*a*) dropped from a height; or

(*b*) subjected to snatch or shock loads.

21.5.2. A sling should not be—

(*a*) used if crossed, twisted, kinked or knotted;

(*b*) used to roll a load over;

(*c*) dragged from beneath a load by a lifting appliance unless the load is resting upon dunnage strips of adequate size; or (*d*) subjected to excessive heat or allowed to come into contact with any acid, alkali or other substance apt to be inimical to the sling.

21.5.3. A shackle should not be used on a sling unless it is fitted with a proper shackle pin; an ordinary bolt or piece of steel bar should not be used.

21.5.4. The links of a chain should not be joined together by a nut and bolt, by wiring, or by passing one link through another and inserting a bolt or nail to hold it in place.

21.5.5. A chain, fibre rope or webbed sling should not be allowed to come into contact with any sharp or jagged edges of the load but should be protected by means of wood or other suitable packing.

21.5.6. (1) Before the hoisting signal is given to the driver of a lifting appliance, it should be ascertained—

(*a*) that the sling is completely free of the load;

(*b*) that, where practicable, any hook or other lifting device at the end of the sling is hooked or attached to the upper ring of the sling.

(2) Where the procedure indicated in subparagraph (*b*) above is not practicable, steps should be taken to ensure that the hook or other lifting device does not catch or foul any fixed object.

21.5.7. (1) No hook or other lifting device should be attached to any wire, strap, band or other fastening of a load unless—

(*a*) it is so attached for the purpose of breaking out in the 'tween decks;

(*b*) setts (drafts) are being made up; or

(*c*) unitised loads are being handled.

(2) In the case of subparagraph (*c*) above, hooks or lifting devices may be so used, provided that—

(*a*) they are specifically designed for the purpose;

(*b*) the wire, strap, band or other fastening has been properly secured to the load;

(*c*) the wire, strap, band or other fastening is compatible with the hook or lifting device being used; and

(*d*) at least two hooks or lifting devices are used, each secured to a separate wire, strap, band or other fastening.

21.5.8. No hook should be attached to the rim or chine of a drum or barrel unless the hook is of suitable shape and unless the rim or chine is of adequate strength and depth for the purpose and is not distorted or otherwise damaged.

21.5.9. No hook should be inserted into the attachment of a load unless the attachment is of sufficient size for the load to be freely supported on the seat of the hook; in no circumstances should the load be applied to the point of the hook or the hook be hammered in.

21.5.10. (1) When lifting a heavy or bulky load, care should be taken not to crowd the hook of the lifting appliance with slings.

(2) If a large number of slings cannot be avoided, one or more shackles should be used to connect the slings to the hook.

21.5.11. (1) When it is necessary to handle irregularly shaped loads such as a machine tool or very long loads where the centre of gravity may be some distance from the vertical geometric centre line, a number of trial lifts should be made by partially lifting the load and adjusting the sling positions until the load, when suspended, is as level as is practicable.

(2) Where it is necessary to shorten one or two legs of a sling in order to achieve equal balance, a proper device such as a chain claw should be used; in no circumstances should the shortening be done by knotting the sling.

21.5.12. (1) When tubes, girders, a long metal sheet or similar long loads are lifted, the safest and most appropriate means should be employed.

(2) Where needed, the load should be fitted with lanyards or guys so that twist or swing of the load may be controlled by persons stationed on the guys.

21.5.13. (1) Unless a load is a sufficient length to warrant the use of a spreader beam or lifting frame, its weight should not exceed—

(*a*) the safe working load of either of the slings when slings of equal safe working loads are used; or

(*b*) the rating of the sling having the lesser safe working load when slings of unequal safe working load are used.

(2) The end of the sling should be passed round the load at least twice before the sling hook is attached to the standing part (choke hitch [1] or snickled) in order to reduce to a minimum the tendency of the slings to slide inwards towards each other when they are under tension.

21.5.14. (1) The weight of a load to be lifted by a sling used in choke hitch should be limited to half the safe working load marked on the sling.

(2) In the case of a sling having an eye at each end and reeved such that both eyes are placed on the hook of the lifting appliance and the two standing parts are reeved through the eye of another sling that has been placed around the load, the weight of the load to be lifted should not be greater than the safe working load marked on either of the slings.

(3) When a chain sling is used in choke hitch, care should be taken to ensure that the hook or eye, as the case may be, is not hooked or reeved into the standing part such that the subtended angle between the standing part and the end of the sling is greater than 120°.[2]

21.5.15. (1) Plate clamps should be of adequate size and strength for the loads handled, and all the teeth on a clamp face and/or locking cam should be sound.

---

[1] i.e. with the end of the sling embracing the load and either the hook being hooked back to the standing part or the eye being reeved in that part.

[2] In the case of a sling other than a chain sling, the sling tends to take up an angle of 120°, but in the case of a chain this is prevented by the hook or eye locking itself in a link of the chain.

(2) Where a plate clamp is used to raise or lower a metal plate by gripping one edge of the plate, with the plate hanging vertically, the clamp should not be directly attached to the hook of the lifting appliance but should be connected to it by a short length of chain: only one plate at a time should be handled in this way.

(3) Where two plate clamps secured to a two-legged sling or two separate slings are used to raise or lower a plate by gripping one edge of the plate, with the plate hanging vertically, the clamps should be applied in such a way that their centre lines are in line with the respective sling legs.

(4) A self-locking plate clamp should not be used unless it is fitted with a safety catch to prevent the load from being accidentally released in the event of the tension upon the clamp becoming momentarily slack.

21.5.16. When a load is lifted by barrel hooks, crate clamps or similar appliances, the sling should be reeved from the crane hook through the barrel hook, crate clamp or similar appliance and then back to the crane hook, in order that the resultant force will tend to make the hook or clamp engage more firmly.

21.5.17. Except when making up a sett in circumstances in which dockworkers could not be injured, the lifting of such loads as bales by the insertion of hooks should be prohibited.

21.5.18. Small loose goods such as small drums, canisters, boxes and carboys should be loaded on to suitable pallets or trays hoisted by four-legged slings; where necessary, special precautions such as fitting a net round the slings should be taken.

21.5.19. Buckets, tubs and similar appliances should—

(*a*) be so loaded that there is no risk of any of the goods falling out;

(*b*) unless fitted with a handle specially designed to fit the hook of a lifting appliance, be secured to the hook by a shackle;

(*c*) have a handle with a special bend at its centre or be so shaped that the hook or shackle will lift the bucket or tub only at the centre of the handle; and (*d*) where the handle is capable of hinging about its attachments to the bucket or tub—

(i) have the hinge points above the centre of gravity of the bucket or tub when it is loaded; and

(ii) have a locking device fitted to prevent the bucket or tub from accidentally turning over when it is suspended.

21.5.20. (1) When a sett of goods such as loaded bags, sacks or reels of paper is to be hoisted—

(*a*) an endless fibre rope sling should be employed, reeved in choke hitch, in such a way that the two parts of the rope encircling the bags or sacks are spaced approximately one-third the length of bag away from each end; or

(*b*) a flat belt sling of adequate width should be used, also rigged in choke hitch.

(2) In the case of paper reels of large diameter, when three reels are hoisted at the same time by means of a sling, the reels should be placed in a triangular fashion, i.e. with one reel resting upon the other two.

(3) The bags or reels should be arranged in such a way that their ends are all approximately in the same vertical plane.

(4) This paragraph should not apply to paper reels that are hoisted by means of a vacuum lifting device, provided that the reels are suitable for this method of hoisting.

21.5.21. When the hook of a multi-legged sling is attached to an eye-fitting on a pallet, tray or load, it should be inserted into the eye from the inside of the load, so that in the event of a leg of the sling becoming momentarily slack, the hook will remain engaged in the eye.

21.5.22. When ingots of metal are hoisted, they should be supported by special bearers having eyes through which the slings are reeved in accordance with the requirements of paragraph 21.5.16, with each layer of ingots being laid at right angles to the layer beneath; or by another suitable and safe method.

21.5.23. When logs are handled—

(*a*) the weight of the log should be based on its being in a saturated condition; only loose gear having a generous excess margin of safe working load should be used;

(*b*) when tongs or scissor clamps are used—

(i) the logs should be at least 1 m shorter than the length of the hatch;

(ii) the tongs should be placed as near as practicable to a point immediately above the centre of gravity of the log, trial lifts being made as necessary for this purpose;

(iii) the tongs should bite into the wood beneath the bark, the bark being removed at the lifting points if there is any doubt whether or not it has been pierced;

(iv) the person applying the tongs should stand well clear when the lift or trial lift is made.

21.5.24. When a reel of cable or coils of metal wire are to be lifted, the slings should be attached to a steel bar of adequate strength and length passing through the hole in the centre of the reel, or through the coils of wire.

21.5.25. Animals, if hoisted, should be loaded and unloaded in boxes, cages or slings that immobilise them sufficiently to prevent dangerous disturbance of loading or unloading operations or injury to dockworkers.

21.6. Raising and lowering loads

21.6.1. A lifting appliance or loose gear should be used only for the purposes for which it is suitable.

21.6.2. A lifting appliance or loose gear should not be loaded beyond the safe working load.

21.6.3. Loads should be raised and lowered smoothly, avoiding sudden jerks.

21.6.4. As far as practicable—

(*a*) loads being raised or lowered should not pass or remain suspended over persons engaged in loading or unloading operations; and

(*b*) no person should pass or stand under a suspended load.

21.6.5. (1) No person should use a hold ladder in the square of a hatch when loads are being raised or lowered in the hold.

(2) As far as practicable, no load should be raised or lowered when any person is using a hold ladder.

21.6.6. Drivers should not leave winches or cranes unattended with a load suspended, or with power on.

21.6.7. (1) When cargo is being loaded or unloaded by a fall at a hatchway, a signaller should be utilised and it should be possible for him to pass safely between hatchway and ship's side.

(2) When more than one fall is being worked at a hatchway, a separate signaller should be utilised for each fall, except in the case of union purchase in which case one signalman should serve each set of gear.

21.6.8. (1) The hoisting, lowering and transporting of loads should be governed by a well understood and uniform code of signals, with a distinctive signal for each operation, preferably by motion of the arms and hands.

(2) Equipment used for giving sound, colour or light signals for hoisting, lowering or transporting loads should be efficient, properly maintained and protected from accidental interference.

21.6.9. (1) Operators of loading and unloading machinery should recognise signals only from designated signallers; provided that every stop signal given in an emergency should be obeyed regardless of who gives it.

(2) The signaller should always be in full view of the winch or crane driver.

21.6.10. Winch or crane drivers should always obey the signaller's signals.

21.6.11. When a load does not ride properly after being hoisted, the signaller should immediately give warning of danger.

21.7. Dragging loads

21.7.1. The use of cranes to drag heavy loads with the crane fall at an angle to the vertical should be prohibited.

21.7.2. (1) Cargo should be dragged with the ship's winches only if the runner is led directly from the derrick heel block so as to avoid overloading the boom and rigging.

(2) Snatch blocks should be used to provide a fair lead for the runner and so prevent it from dragging against obstructions.

(3) When dragging cargo, special precautions should be taken to ensure that all dock workers are clear of the lines and are not standing in the bight of a rope, and that competent supervision is provided.

21.7.3. Cranes and ships' winches should not be used to move lighters, other vessels' rail cars or other vehicles; unless the runner is properly rigged so as to give a direct line to the winch drum or whipping drum (gipsy head).

21.8. Grabs

21.8.1. When bulk goods are moved with grabs—

(*a*) there should be ample room for workers at loading and unloading points to avoid the swinging grab;

(*b*) grabs should be secured against inadvertent opening and be so constructed that they can be locked in the open position to prevent persons from being trapped by accidental closing; and

(*c*) if heavy goods such as ore are being handled, special supervision should be provided for trimmers.

21.9. Magnets

21.9.1. Lifting magnets should be used in holds only when dock-workers are able to take shelter from any falling pieces.

21.10. Working with whipping drums

21.10.1. When cargo is worked by using a runner wound round a winch whipping drum, an operator should be constantly stationed at the winch controls to stop the winch immediately in case of need; while so stationed, he should perform no other work.

21.11. Loading and unloading rafts

21.11.1. Rafts used for loading should be of sufficient size and bearing capacity.

21.11.2. Safety lines and lifebuoys, and when necessary a boat, should be readily available.

22. Flat belt slings

22.1. General provisions

22.1.1. For general use, the width of the belt should not be greater than 30 cm or less than 50 mm; however, purpose-designed slings of width greater than 30 cm are not precluded.

22.1.2. The minimum length of a soft eye measured internally when the belt is laid flat should not be less than 22.5 cm.

22.1.3. The sling should be made of man-made fibre; if the sling is treated with any substance with the object of increasing its resistance to abrasion, the substance should be compatible with the man-made fibre used.

22.1.4. Where the sling is likely to be exposed to prolonged bright sunshine, the material should be suitably stabilised against degradation by ultra-violet light.

22.1.5. The stitching material should be of the same man-made yarn as the sling and the join should be such that, so far as is practicable, the load is distributed equally across the width of the belt.

22.1.6. The sling should be made to an approved manufacturer's standard, including quality control and reliability tests of samples taken from production batches.

22.1.7. The manufacturer or his accredited supplier should supply with each sling or batch of the same type of sling a certificate incorporating the following items:

(*a*) a declaration that the sling will not break at less than six times its safe working load;

(*b*) the safe working load of the sling in straight lift;

(*c*) the distinguishing mark of each sling to relate it to the certificate;

(*d*) the belt and stitching material from which the sling is made; and

(*e*) a mark to indicate that it has been made to an approved standard.

22.1.8. Any end fitting should comply with the relevant requirements of Chapter 20.

22.1.9. The belt sling and its end fitting, where appropriate, should be marked in accordance with the requirements of section 20.6.

22.2. Precautions during use

22.2.1. In addition to the precautions indicated in paragraphs 21.4.1, 21.5.2, 21.5.5, 21.5.6, 21.5.10, 21.5.11, 21.5.13 and 21.5.14 and section 10.5, the following precautions should be observed:

(*a*) when used with another sling to form a two-legged sling, the angle between the two legs should be diminished as the width of the sling increases; in general the included angle between them should not be greater than 60° for slings up to 15 cm in width; for widths above 15 cm a spreader beam should always be used;

(*b*) during the inspection required under subparagraph 20.2.1(*d*), particular care should be taken to look for chafe, cross or longitudinal cuts in the belting (particularly at the edge of the belting) and damage to the stitched joint.

22.3. Disposable flat belt slings

22.3.1. (1) A disposable sling should comply with the requirements of section 22.1, except in the following respects:

(*a*) the width of the belt should not be less than 25 mm;

(*b*) the declaration required under subparagraph 22.1.7(*a*) should state that the sling will not break at less than five times its safe working load in the case of a belt width of 25 mm up to 50 mm and at less than four times its safe working load in the case of a belt width of 50 mm and above.

(2) The sling should be marked in a suitable place, in such a way

that will remain legible throughout the life of the sling, with the following information:

(*a*) its safe working load from 0° to 60°;

(*b*) either the mark "U", indicating a disposable sling, or the word "disposable" in English and the language of the country where it will be taken off the load;

(*c*) the maker's identification;

(*d*) a batch number including reference to its year of manufacture.

22.3.2. A sling marked in accordance with the requirements of subparagraph 22.3.1(2) should—

(*a*) not be used to raise a load if its angle to the vertical is less than 60°;

(*b*) be scrapped by cutting up or other suitable means after it has been taken from its load at the final destination.

23. Stacking and storage of goods

23.1. General provisions

23.1.1. The method of stacking or storage of goods should be determined by—

(*a*) the availability of mechanical handling equipment;

(*b*) the length of the transit period; and

(*c*) the space available.

23.1.2. Where possible, cargo should be arranged—

(*a*) as complete pallet loads; or

(*b*) on pallet racking.

23.1.3. When locating storage areas, consideration should be given to—

(*a*) permissible floor loading in buildings; and

(*b*) the presence of underground sewers or culverts.

23.1.4. Stacks of stored goods should be broken down systematically from the top tier in order to ensure stability of the main body of the stack.

23.1.5. (1) The shape and relative fragility of the article should be considered when the stack is being built up.

(2) Long thin articles (other than timber) should be stored in horizontal racks.

(3) Box-shaped articles should be built into a stack with suitable bonding.

(4) Cylindrical articles may be stored on end or on their sides.

(5) When cylindrical articles are stored on their sides, the floor-level tier should be properly chocked to prevent movement.

23.1.6. (1) Dunnage should be used as appropriate under articles that are to be loaded or unloaded by fork-lift trucks or other lifting devices.

(2) Dunnage should be of sufficient size to allow the forks or slings to be inserted or removed.

23.2. Loose material stored in bunkers, bins, hoppers, silos or similar places

23.2.1. (1) A new storage place should be designed to be self-cleaning, i.e. with the sides so smooth and at such an angle that the material will not cling.

(2) Vibratory devices should be fitted either in the material or to the sides of the storage place (where these are of suitable construction) to ensure that the material flows readily.

23.2.2. (1) Where a person is required to enter a storage place and stand on the cargo to clear a blockage, a permit-to-enter system should be arranged.

(2) The person should wear a suitable safety harness connected to one or two lifelines, according to circumstances; if two lifelines are used they should be held by two persons situated on opposite sides of the storage place.

(3) The lifelines should be kept as taut as practicable and where possible belayed at suitable positions in order that, if the person loses his foothold or if the material collapses owing to the presence of a cavity below the surface on which he is standing, his weight is immediately supported.

(4) The safety harness and lifelines should be kept in a suitable place and be thoroughly examined before each occasion of use.

23.3. Timber

23.3.1. Stacks should whenever possible be built up of pieces of timber of similar length.

23.3.2. Each layer should rest upon dunnage placed at right angles to the pieces of timber.

23.3.3. The practice of leaving staggered plank ends protruding from the face of stacks in order that persons may climb up should not be permitted.

23.3.4. In the case of timber of relatively short length, each layer should be stacked at right angles to the layer below in order to make the stack self-binding, and the height of the stack should be restricted.

23.3.5. (1) Logs or round timber should where practicable be stacked in such a way that the larger diameter material is in the lower tier, with each higher layer being of smaller diameter, in order to obtain a pyramid effect.

(2) These stacks should be retained by special frames or by chocks of special design, adequate in strength and size, or by other similarly effective devices.

23.4. Paper pulp

23.4.1. (1) The stack should not generally be more than 20 bales in height.

(2) The bales should be bonded by stacking each layer with bales, the longer sides of which are at right angles to the bales in the tier below.

(3) The spacing between the bales in the bottom tier should be as much as possible, the spacing being slightly reduced in each succeeding tier, in order to obtain a pyramid effect.

(4) Adequate air spaces should be left to avoid the danger of spontaneous combustion.

23.5. Paper reels, drums, etc.

23.5.1. (1) Where stacking is carried out by means of a lifting appliance fitted with drum or squeeze clamps (paragraph 19.5.3), the reels or drums may be stacked on end.

(2) The reels or drums should be of the same diameter.

(3) The height of the stack should be limited by such considerations as the diameter and weight of the reels or drums.

(4) Where possible, drums, particularly when empty, should be stored on pallets.

23.5.2. When reels or drums are stored in the horizontal position, the requirements of paragraph 23.3.5 should be complied with.

23.6. Steel sheets and plates

23.6.1. Where the sheets are packaged and are of limited size and weight, they may be stacked upon each other to a height not exceeding 2 m, the bundles being separated by suitable dunnage.

23.6.2. (1) When individual sheets of appreciable weight are stacked in toast-rack fashion, i.e. on edge, they should lean against vertical supports of adequate strength and be on a solid foundation.

(2) Plates stored in this fashion should be handled by self-locking plate cams.

23.7. Coiled steel sheet

23.7.1. (1) Coiled steel sheet may be stacked in nesting tiers, i.e. with coils in the tier above resting in the hollows formed by the tier below.

(2) The tier at floor level should be firmly chocked to prevent horizontal displacement.

(3) The considerable weight of the coils should be borne in mind.

(4) If the coils are of varying diameter, they should be stacked in descending order of size with coils of the largest diameter being at floor level.

(5) The height of the stack should be limited to not more than five tiers.

23.8. Storage racks

23.8.1. (1) All storage racks should be of good construction and of adequate strength and, in particular, should be properly cross-braced.

(2) The height/base ratio will depend upon the construction of the rack and the weight and nature of the goods contained.

23.9. Deck cargo handling

23.9.1. (1) All upper decks to which dockworkers may have access for the purpose of carrying on dock work should be provided on the outer edge with a bulwark or guard rails so designed, constructed and placed, and of such a height above the deck, as to prevent any worker from accidentally falling overboard.

(2) The bulwark or guard rails should be continuous except where sections have to be removed; such sections should not extend beyond the minimum distance necessary.

(3) Removable sections should be securely fastened when in position.

23.9.2. (1) Valves, drain cocks and flange connections of steam pipes should be maintained in good condition.

(2) Any escape of steam should be immediately reported to the ship's officers, who should at once take the necessary remedial measures.

23.9.3. (1) Deck cargoes should be stowed, or effective measures taken, so that—

(*a*) safe access is provided to the winches and hold ladders and to the signaller's stand; and

(*b*) if the winches are to be used during loading or unloading, they can be safely operated.

(2) Safe access to the deck cargo, hold ladders and winches should be ensured by securely installed steps or ladders.

23.9.4. When a signaller has to move from the square of the hatch to the ship's side, a space at least 1 m wide should be kept clear.

23.9.5. If the surface of the deck cargo is uneven, safe gang-planks running both fore and aft and thwartships should be provided where practicable.

23.9.6. When deck cargo that is not being worked is stowed against ships' rails or hatch coamings, and at such a height that the rails or coamings would not prevent dockworkers from falling over-board or into the open hold, temporary fencing should be provided.

23.9.7. (1) Where cargo is stowed on deck or in the 'tween decks and the hatches have to be opened at intermediate ports before that cargo is unloaded, it should be so stowed as to provide a clear space of at least 1 m around the coamings or around the part of the hatch that is to be opened at following ports.

(2) If this is impracticable, such provision should be made, as for example fencing or lifelines, as will enable dockworkers to remove and replace in safety all fore and aft beams and thwartship beams used for hatch covering and all hatch coverings.

(3) The coaming clearance of 1 m should be marked with a painted line.

23.9.8. If goods have to be stowed on hatch covers—

(*a*) due regard should be paid to the bearing capacity of the covers;

(*b*) the responsible persons should satisfy themselves that the hatch beams are properly placed and the hatch covers sit well and fit tight together; and

(*c*) the responsible persons should satisfy themselves that the hatch beams and hatch covers are in an undamaged condition.

23.9.9. When a deck cargo is carried, adequate arrangements should be made to ensure that the signaller is seen by the crane or winch driver.

23.10. Lifting and carrying material

23.10.1. Where reasonable and practicable, mechanical appliances should be provided and used for lifting and carrying loads.

23.10.2. Workers assigned to handling loads should be instructed in techniques of lifting and carrying safely.[1]

23.10.3. No person should be employed to lift, carry or move any load so heavy as to be likely to cause injury to him.[1]

23.10.4. Where heavy objects, such as loaded drums or tanks, are handled on inclines in either direction—

(*a*) ropes or other tackle should be used to control their motion, in addition to the necessary chocks or wedges; and

(*b*) workers should not stand on the downhill side.

23.10.5. Where heavy objects are moved by means of rollers, bars or sledges should be used instead of hands and feet for changing the direction of the rollers while in motion.

23.10.6. Lifting jacks of all types should be of such construction that the load—

(*a*) will remain supported in any position; and

(*b*) cannot be lowered unintentionally.

23.10.7. When objects are lifted with jacks, the jacks should be—

(*a*) set on solid footings;

(*b*) centred properly for the lifts; and

(*c*) so placed that they can be operated without obstruction.

23.10.8. Workers handling objects with sharp edges, fins, slivers, splinters or similar dangerous projecting parts, or handling hot or corrosive materials, should be provided with and should use suitable

---

1 For full details see the ILO Maximum Weight Convention, 1967 (No.127), and Maximum Weight Recommendation, 1967 (No. 128), concerning the maximum permissible weight to be carried by one worker.

protective clothing and equipment in accordance with the relevant requirements of Chapter 27.

23.10.9. Workers handling cases should beware of nails, sharp points, splinters and metal bands.

23.11. Pallets—general provisions

23.11.1. Pallets, including expendable pallets, should comply with the requirements of subparagraph 4.2.1(*a*) to (*d*).

23.11.2. When pallets are selected, care should be taken to ensure that they are of adequate strength; in particular, load distribution, handling and storage methods should be considered.

23.11.3. Re-usable pallets should be fitted with fastenings in the form of bolts and nuts, drive screws (helically threaded nails), annular threaded nails or fastenings of equivalent strength.

23.11.4. Wing- or lip-type pallets hoisted by means of bar bridles should have an overhanging wing or lip at least 75 mm long.

23.12. Use of pallets

23.12.1. (1) Before being loaded with goods, pallets should be inspected to ensure that they are in a safe condition.

(2) All damaged pallets should be withdrawn for repair or destruction.

23.12.2. Empty pallets should—

(*a*) be carefully handled and not dragged or thrown down; and

(*b*) not be handled by such methods as wedging the platform of a sack barrow between the top and bottom deck boards.

23.12.3. (1) Pallets should be loaded with goods to an established pattern designed to achieve maximum stability within the rated load of the pallet.

(2) As a general guide, the height of the load should not exceed the longest base dimension.

(3) Loads should be applied gradually and, unless the pallet has been specifically designed for point loading, goods should as far as possible be uniformly distributed.

23.12.4. (1) If pallets are to be stacked, a firm level base on the floor or deck or on top of the preceding pallet should be provided.

(2) Generally, loaded pallets should not be stacked more than four high.

(3) Pallets should not be stacked in racking unless they are suitable for this method of storage.

23.12.5. Care should be exercised when strapping is used to secure loads to pallets.[1]

23.12.6. The forks of handling machines should extend into the pallet a distance that is equivalent to at least 75 per cent of the dimension of the pallet parallel to the forks, and the forks should be so spaced that the maximum support is given to the pallet when it is lifted.

23.12.7. If pallet trucks are used, care should be taken to ensure that the small finger wheels do not cause damage to the base boards.

23.12.8. Pallets handled by crane should be lifted only by suitable fork attachments or, in the case of wing pallets, by bar slings with spreaders.

23.12.9. Loaded pallets which, on visual examination, do not meet the requirements of this section should, before being handled, be placed on pallets that do meet those requirements.

23.12.10. (1) Extreme caution should be exercised when pallets are re-used.[2]

(2) Expendable or disposable pallets should not be re-used.

---

[1] Because deck boards can be pulled from the bearers if excessive strap tension is used.

[2] Because a change of goods or handling methods may give rise to loads for which the pallet was not designed.

23.13. Inspection of pallets for damage

23.13.1. When inspecting pallets for damage, the following danger points should be watched for:

(*a*) on old pallets—

(i) damaged bearers or stringers;

(ii) split or displaced blocks;

(iii) projecting nails or nails pulled through deck boards;

(iv) damaged deck boards, particularly leading-edge boards;

(v) loose boards permitting the pallet to distort or rack;

(*b*) on new pallets—

(i) distorted or split bearers or stringers;

(ii) split blocks;

(iii) badly spaced or split deck boards;

(iv) badly spaced or projecting nails;

(v) extensive bark or knot inclusions in any member.

24. Warehouses

24.1. General provisions

24.1.1. The floor of any warehouse should comply with the requirements of section 2.1 so far as appropriate.

24.1.2. (1) Stacks should be laid out in an orderly fashion with aisles of sufficient width to permit the safe use of fork-lift trucks and other vehicles handling goods.

(2) The aisles should be clearly marked by continuous yellow lines.

24.1.3. So far as is practicable—

(*a*) a system of one-way traffic or a circular route should be established and be clearly indicated by signs;

(*b*) main traffic lanes should be clearly marked;

(*c*) traffic should be properly controlled; and

(*d*) traffic lanes should be kept clear of obstructions such as cargo, dunnage, gear and equipment.

24.1.4. Where pedestrian lanes cross traffic lines, suitable warning signs should be posted for both pedestrians and vehicle drivers and the crossing should be marked with alternating black and yellow stripes.

24.1.5. (1) The maximum load per unit area to be carried by any floor and the maximum gross weight of any vehicle that may be used on any such floor should be marked.

(2) These maximum loads should not be exceeded.

24.1.6. When work is proceeding on a high stack, warning notices should be displayed and adequate measures taken for the safety of persons passing below.

24.1.7. (1) Where there is danger from overhead bare crane conductor wires, from other electrical equipment, or of trapping by overhead gantries, these hazards should either be properly guarded against or the height of the stack should be limited to the extent necessary to avoid the danger.

(2) Precautions should be taken to ensure that any person using a portable ladder, particularly a ladder made of metal, does not place it in such a position that it is, or he is, apt to come into contact with overhead bare electric conductors (see also paragraph 3.4.9).

24.2. Access to top of stack

24.2.1. (1) Safe means of access should be provided to the top of a stack.

(2) Where a ladder is used to provide access to the top of a stack—

(*a*) it should comply with the requirements of section 3.4;

(*b*) it should be so placed that the person gaining access can step safely from the ladder to the top of the stack; and

(*c*) the person should take particular care when stepping from the ladder on to goods such as bales of paper pulp that may wobble or give under his weight.

24.2.2. No person should be permitted to ascend or descend from a stack on the forks of a fork-lift truck or other part of a lifting appliance, except that a crane may be used for this purpose if—

(*a*) it is provided with a safety chair suitable for the purpose and secured to the hook in such a way that it is not liable to become displaced;

(*b*) the overwinding limit switch of the crane provided in accordance with the requirements of section 4.11 is tested by the driver of the crane before the chair is used for the first time on any working day or shift;

(*c*) the person is raised clear of the stack or any part of the building such as roof supports, crane stanchions and any overhead bare electric conductors;

(*d*) the crane does not traverse or slew except to the extent necessary to deposit the person on the stack at a safe distance from any edge;

(*e*) the driver of the crane obeys only signals given by the person riding in the chair, other than an emergency stop call from any person; and

(*f*) the hook is secured to the hoist rope of the crane by means of a wedge socket fitting, which should comply with the requirements of paragraph 9.6.2.

24.3. Floor or wall openings

24.3.1. (1) Every opening in a floor or wall should either be covered or protected by means of—

(*a*) a guard rail fitted not less than 1 m above the floor level; and

(*b*) where there is danger of a person or objects passing beneath the guard rail, a toe board not less than 15 cm in height above the floor level.

(2) The guard rail and, where fitted, the toe board may be removed to the extent necessary for the passage of goods.

24.4. Ventilation

24.4.1. Where trucks powered by internal combustion engines are used, adequate arrangements should be made for ventilation and removal of the exhaust fumes.

24.5. Compliance with other regulations

24.5.1. All regulations adopted by the administration of the country in respect of the following should be complied with:

(*a*) fire precautions, including means of escape in case of fire;

(*b*) any lift used by persons employed in the warehouse;

(*c*) the construction of the building, in particular the strength and suitability of mezzanine and other floors used for storage of goods and, where appropriate, the use of trucks; and

(*d*) stairways, etc.

24.6. Maintenance

24.6.1. Warehouses and storeplaces should be maintained in a safe condition, and any dangerous conditions found in floors, steps, galleries, stairs, hoist hatches, etc., should be immediately remedied.

25. Dock railways

25.1. General provisions

25.1.1. Dock railways should be constructed, equipped, maintained and operated in accordance with the relevant provisions of safety rules governing railways of the national system.

25.1.2. Sufficient clearance to ensure safety should be allowed between structures or piles of material and railway tracks.

25.1.3. Where buildings have doorways opening directly on to dock railway tracks, at blind corners or at other places where the field of vision is particularly restricted, workers should be protected against stepping on to the tracks in front of moving vehicles by suitable warning signs and, where practicable, by fixed detour railings across the direct path so installed as to ensure safe clearance for trainmen riding on cars.

25.1.4. Ground levers working points should be so placed that persons working them are clear of adjacent lines and as little obstruction as possible is caused to persons employed.

25.1.5. Where necessary to prevent danger, point rods and signal wires should be sufficiently covered or otherwise guarded.

25.1.6. Warning signs and obstruction guards on dock railways should be made conspicuous by painting, for example with alternating black and yellow stripes.

25.1.7. Where dock railways are operated during hours of darkness, all warning signs and obstruction guards should be illuminated.

25.1.8. Locomotive drivers should act only on signals given by an authorised person; provided that stop signals should always be acted on, irrespective of their source.

25.1.9. Locomotive warning devices should be actuated before setting standing locomotives or trains in motion and when approaching level crossings and particularly hazardous places.

25.1.10. Unauthorised persons should not ride on locomotives or railway cars.

25.1.11. Locomotives pulling or pushing cars should move dead slow and should be preceded by a man on foot when passing through a dock area where men are working.

25.1.12. Workers should not pass under or between railway vehicles.

25.2. Loading and unloading

25.2.1. When opening car doors, workers should take care—

(*a*) to see that fastenings are in good order; and

(*b*) to keep clear of the door and of any goods that might fall out of the car.

25.2.2. Workers should not be inside gondola cars (open wagons) when—

(*a*) bulk material is being handled by means of grabs; or

(*b*) metal stock is being handled by means of magnetic lifting devices.

25.2.3. Where gondola cars with swinging side doors are being emptied near passageways or walkways, danger signs should be placed at either end of the exposed sections.

25.2.4. When drop doors on gondola cars with hopper bottoms or on hopper cars are opened, precautions should be taken to prevent workers' fingers from being crushed.

25.2.5. Car plates (gangplanks) should—

(*a*) be strong enough to carry safely the maximum load for which they are used;

(*b*) be provided with positive stops to prevent shifting;

(*c*) have non-skid bearing surfaces;

(*d*) be provided with toe boards at least 15 cm high at the sides;

(*e*) have the maximum bearing capacity conspicuously marked on them;

(*f*) be provided with an appropriate device by which they can be lifted and moved;

(*g*) be properly secured; and

(*h*) when not in use, be so stored as not to create a hazard.

25.2.6. Suitable tools should be provided and used for the unfastening of metal straps.

25.2.7. No lift trucks should be used inside railway cars unless the floor of the car is in a safe condition for the purpose.

25.2.8. When workers are required to work between or beneath railway cars, they should be provided with a look-out man responsible for giving them any necessary warnings concerning movements of vehicles, etc.

25.2.9. When double-deck cars are being used—

(*a*) a handrail should be provided around the top deck; and

(*b*) walkways adjacent to the handrail should have a non-slip surface.

25.3. Moving of cars

25.3.1. Flying switches (shunts) in areas where dock work is being carried on should be prohibited, and all trains should be brought to a full stop before any cars are cut loose.

25.3.2. (1) Where it is necessary to move railway cars more than a short distance without a locomotive, the cars should be shifted by means of—

(*a*) power-driven car movers; or

(*b*) manually or mechanically operated winches or capstans.

(2) Cars should move dead slow and be preceded by a man on foot when passing through a dock area where men are working.

25.3.3. (1) When cars are being moved by capstans, workers

should keep clear of the hauling rope and not stand between the rope and the cars.

(2) The space immediately around the capstan should be kept free of all obstructions.

(3) The controls of the capstan should be on the side away from the hauling rope.

(4) Capstan controls should be such that the operator is clear of the intake of the rope.

(5) If capstans are treadle operated, the treadle should be tested before each day of use.

25.3.4. (1) Wherever practicable, the moving of railway cars on adjacent tracks or on cross-overs by means of push poles between locomotives and cars should be avoided.

(2) Where push poles are used for moving railway cars with locomotives on adjacent tracks, the workers handling the poles should face the direction of the motion so that the poles will move away from them.

25.3.5. When a railway car or a group of cars not directly connected to a locomotive is being moved, a worker should be appointed to control each car or group of cars.

25.3.6. As far as practicable, idle cars should not be left standing on quays with short distances between them.

25.3.7. Before moving railway cars, train crews should make sure that all dockworkers are out of the cars and the danger zone.

25.3.8. Cranes, ships' winches and derricks should not be used to move railway cars.

25.3.9. Before cars are moved, hinged doors should be properly fastened and all insecure and overhanging stanchions or metal straps in the car should be removed and placed away from any working area.

26. Dangerous substances and environments

26.1. Handling of dangerous substances

26.1.1. Explosives, highly flammable liquids and other dangerous substances should be loaded, unloaded, handled and stored in accordance with the relevant requirements of national or local regulations, due account being taken of applicable national and international standards such as those of the Inter-Governmental Maritime Consultative Organisation.

26.1.2. (1) Dangerous substances should be loaded, unloaded, handled and stored only under the supervision of a competent person who is familiar with the risks and the precautions to be taken.

(2) In case of doubt as to the nature of the risk or the precautions to be taken, the necessary instructions should be obtained from the competent authority.

26.1.3. (1) Dangerous substances should not be loaded, unloaded, handled or stored unless they are packed and labelled in compliance with national or international regulations for the transport of such substances.

(2) In the case of bulk cargo where labelling may present difficulties, the necessary indications should be given on the bill of lading or other ship's document.

26.1.4. (1) Prior to the start of cargo-handling operations, it should be ascertained from the labels on the cargo, from the dangerous cargo manifest or from other shipping documents, what hazardous cargoes, if any, are to be handled and the general nature of the hazard.

(2) Dockworkers should be informed of the general nature of the hazard, the importance of not damaging the cargo and any special precautions to be taken.

(3) Dockworkers should report any damaged containers, leaks or spills.

(4) Where practicable, the previous cargo in a hold or compartment should be determined and it should be ascertained that the hold or compartment has been properly cleaned or ventilated prior to the start of loading operations.

26.1.5. Special precautions, such as the provision of mats, sling nets, boxes and high-sided pallets, should be taken to prevent breakage of or damage to containers of dangerous substances.

26.1.6. (1) If a cargo, which has been determined to be hazardous, is spilled or any of its contents has or develops a serious leak, dockworkers should be removed from the hold or compartment to a safe place until—

(*a*) the specific hazard has been ascertained;

(*b*) proper personal protective equipment and clothing has been provided;

(*c*) ventilation and fire protective equipment sufficient to avoid or protect dockworkers against the hazard has been provided; and

(*d*) the dockworkers have been informed as to the safe method of cleaning up and disposing of the spill and disposing of the leaking containers.

(2) The actual work of cleaning up or disposal should be carried out under the supervision of an experienced person.

26.1.7. (1) Explosive substances should not be left on quays or other dock areas longer than necessary.

(2) If explosive substances have to be left on quays or other dock areas, the competent authority should prescribe the maximum quantity in the respective risk categories that may be so left and the distances to be maintained between the explosive substances and buildings, ships, other goods, etc., with due regard to the risk category and the quantity of the explosive substances.

(3) Where dangerous liquids in bulk are loaded, all pumps,

pipelines, flexible hoses and connections and all lifting and supporting equipment used in conjunction with them should be of good construction, made of sound and suitable materials, free from defects and properly maintained.

26.1.8. Where there is an explosion risk, all electrical equipment and circuits should be made dead and kept dead as long as the risk lasts, unless such equipment and circuits are safe for use in the circumstances in question.

26.1.9. When highly flammable cargo is being loaded or unloaded, special measures should be taken to ensure that an incipient fire can be controlled immediately.

26.1.10. In order to reduce the hazard from sparking, adequate precautions should be taken when hand tools are used—

(*a*) on vessels that carry oil, liquefied combustible gases or other flammable liquids;

(*b*) near flammable or explosive material; and

(*c*) in the presence of explosive dusts or vapours.

26.1.11. Before fumigated cargo such as grain is loaded or unloaded, adequate measures should be taken to ensure that the cargo is safe to handle.

26.1.12. Where corrosive substances are handled or stored, special precautions should be taken to prevent damage to the containers and to render any spillage harmless.

26.1.13. Where necessary, dockworkers loading or unloading or otherwise handling dangerous substances should be provided with and use protective clothing and personal protective equipment in accordance with the relevant requirements of section 27.1.

26.1.14. Dockworkers should not touch dead rats, but should remove them with tongs or other suitable means.

26.1.15. Dockworkers handling harmful substances should thoroughly wash their hands and face with soap or some other suitable cleaning agent before taking any food or drink.

26.1.16. If skins, wool, hair, bones or other animal parts have not been certified by a competent authority as having been disinfected, in particular against anthrax, or in cases where a risk of infection is suspected, the workers concerned should—

(*a*) be instructed in the risks of infection and the precautions to be taken, for example by cautionary notices and leaflets;

(*b*) be provided with and use personal protective equipment in accordance with the relevant requirements of section 27.1; and

(*c*) be subject to special medical supervision.

26.2. Dangerous and harmful environments

26.2.1. (1) Where, in the course of loading or unloading, any dust or fibre is given off to such an extent as to be likely to injure health or to cause explosions, mechanical handling methods should be used as far as possible to reduce exposure of dockworkers to such hazard.

(2) Where dockworkers are exposed to dangerous or irritating concentrations of dust, suitable respiratory protective equipment should be supplied and worn.

26.2.2. When there is danger from broken or leaking containers of dangerous substances, dockworkers should be evacuated from the area involved and the following steps taken before work is resumed:

(*a*) if the cargo is one which produces dangerous gases or vapours—

(i) suitable respiratory protective equipment should be readily available for dockworkers who are to remove the defective containers;

(ii) suitable rescue equipment and persons trained in its use should be readily available for the purpose of rescuing dockworkers who have been overcome; and

(iii) the area should be ventilated if necessary, and tested to ensure that the concentration of gases or vapours in the atmosphere is not high enough to be dangerous;

(*b*) if the cargo is a corrosive substance—

(i) suitable protective clothing should be readily available to protect dockworkers engaged in the removal of damaged containers; and

(ii) suitable absorbent or neutralising materials should be used in cleaning up the spillage.

26.2.3. (1) Where internal combustion engines are used for loading or unloading operations in holds or confined spaces—

(*a*) the operator should not work alone, unless circumstances are such that the operator is under frequent observation by others;

(*b*) at any working place, particularly under the overheads, care should be taken that there is no harmful concentration of carbon monoxide or other exhaust gases; and

(*c*) if adequate ventilation is not ensured by natural means or the ventilation equipment of the ship, additional mechanical ventilation should be provided.

(2) Roll-on-roll-off ships should be equipped with a permanently installed, automatic carbon monoxide monitoring equipment, covering all compartments and giving an audible and visual warning of a build-up of carbon monoxide above the limits established by the national authority.

26.2.4. Before dockworkers are permitted to enter enclosed spaces, tanks, etc., in which fermentation of organic material or rusting may have resulted in a deficiency of oxygen, such spaces should be tested by suitable means, such as a flame safety lamp, to ascertain whether there is sufficient oxygen.

26.2.5. (1) Before dockworkers are permitted to work in a hold, space or intermodal container which has been fumigated, the hold, space or intermodal container should be certified safe by a competent person.

(2) Where holds or intermodal containers are refrigerated by the use of nitrogen gas, no person should be allowed to enter prior to ventilation and testing.

26.2.6. (1) Dry ice should not be used below deck.

(2) If dry ice has been used in holds or confined spaces for refrigeration, suitable tests should be made before dockworkers are allowed to enter such places.

26.2.7. Adequate measures, such as additional ventilation and the provision of saline drinks, should be taken where necessary to prevent heat exhaustion.

26.2.8. Where dockworkers are employed in abnormal environments, where there are extremes of temperature or where the wearing of respiratory equipment is essential, they should be relieved at suitable intervals for rest in fresh air.

26.3. Tankers

26.3.1. Tankers should be loaded and unloaded in conformity with the relevant requirements of national regulations or the competent authority.

26.4. Noise

26.4.1. (1) Where the noise level, either in the cab of a vehicle or in the hold or a combination of both, is sufficiently high as to be apt to impair the hearing of any person, that person should be issued with suitable ear-muffs.

(2) As soon as possible after the unloading or loading of a deck of a ship has commenced, a responsible person having the necessary knowledge and experience of the use of noise-measuring meters should check the noise level on the deck at a suitable number of representative positions both inside and outside vehicle cabs.

(3) When the noise level exceeds a predetermined limit, the driver and other persons concerned should wear protective equipment.

(4) The procedure in subparagraphs (2) and (3) need not be carried out in the case of vehicles regularly used on ships that regularly visit the dock and where the noise levels are known and the necessary precautions have been taken as may be necessary.

27. Personal protective equipment

27.1. General provisions

27.1.1. (1) Where other means of protection against harmful agents are impracticable or insufficient, dockworkers should be provided with adequate protective clothing and personal protective equipment to shield them from the effects of such agents.

(2) Protective clothing and personal protective equipment should at least conform to any national standards that may be applicable.

27.1.2. Dockworkers should be instructed in the use of protective clothing and personal protective equipment provided.

27.1.3. Dockworkers should make proper use of, and take proper care of, the protective clothing and personal protective equipment provided.

27.1.4. Protective clothing and equipment should be cleaned at suitable intervals and properly maintained.

27.1.5. Where protective clothing and equipment may be contaminated by poisonous or other dangerous substances, it should be stored in separate accommodation where it will not contaminate the workers' clothing.

27.1.6. Before being issued, personal protective equipment that comes into contact with the skin should be washed and disinfected.

27.1.7. Suitable protection for the skin, such as barrier creams and coverings, should be provided when there is a risk of the skin coming into contact with materials having an injurious or penetrative effect on it.

27.1.8. Suitable protection, such as disinfectants and skin coverings, should be provided against the danger of infection when parts of animals which may be infected are handled.

27.1.9. Suitable breathing apparatus, helmets or respirators acceptable to the competent authority should be provided as protection against the inhalation of poisonous or corrosive fumes, gases, vapours or dust.

27.1.10. Suitable appliances such as goggles, masks or screens should be provided as protection against the penetration of harmful fumes, gases, vapours, dust, fragments, etc., into the eyes.

27.1.11. On work with which there is a risk of corrosive or heat burns, suitable protective equipment such as gloves, gaiters and aprons should be provided.

27.1.12. When goods liable to cause injuries are handled, suitable protective equipment such as gloves, tongs, neck leathers, top boots and protective hats should be provided and worn.

27.1.13. Dockworkers should as far as practicable wear safety footwear while at work.

27.1.14. Suitable protective clothing should be provided for work in refrigerated spaces.

28. Medical aid

28.1. General provisions

28.1.1. Except in emergencies, first aid in case of accident or sudden illness should be rendered only by a medical doctor, a nurse or a person trained in first aid and possessing a first-aid certificate acceptable to the competent authority.

28.1.2. Adequate means and personnel for rendering first aid should be readily available during working hours at places where dock work is carried on.

28.1.3. Severely injured persons should not be moved before the arrival of a doctor or other qualified person except for the purpose of removing them from a dangerous place.

28.1.4. All injuries, however slight, should be reported as soon as possible to the nearest first-aid man or room.

28.2. First-aid boxes

28.2.1. One or more first-aid boxes should be provided at suitable places near workplaces and be protected against contamination by dust, moisture, etc.

28.2.2. (1) First-aid boxes should contain adequate material for rendering first aid to dockworkers.

(2) The contents of first-aid boxes should comply with the relevant provisions of national regulations or standards.

(3) First-aid boxes should not contain anything beside material for first aid.

28.2.3. First-aid boxes should contain simple and clear instructions to be followed in emergencies.

28.2.4. First-aid boxes should if necessary be replenished after each occasion of use.

28.2.5. (1) First-aid boxes should be in the charge of a responsible person who is qualified to render first aid.

(2) The contents and condition of every first-aid box should be inspected at least once a month by the person in charge of it.

28.3. Stretchers

28.3.1. (1) Stretchers, so constructed and equipped that persons can be hoisted from a hold in a safe manner and be further transported without having to be transferred from the stretcher, should be readily available.

(2) Two clean blankets should be provided for each stretcher.

28.4. Injuries from corrosive substances

28.4.1. Where dockworkers are exposed to the risk of injury from corrosive substances—

(*a*) suitable first-aid facilities such as eye-wash bottles and means of drenching with water should be provided and kept readily available; and

(*b*) notices giving suitable first-aid instructions should be displayed.

28.5. Rescue from drowning

28.5.1. (1) Suitable means for the treatment of persons rescued from drowning should be readily available (see also section 2.5).

(2) The means of rescue should include an adequate number of lifebuoys with an adequate length of line attached, boat hooks, grapnels and ladders of suitable length.

28.6. Presence of first-aid men

28.6.1. If dock work is carried out by ten or more dockworkers on a ship not lying moored to the shore, or by 25 or more dockworkers elsewhere, at least one person who is qualified to render first aid should be present.

28.7. Boats

28.7.1. If dock work is carried out on a ship that is not in direct communication with the shore during working hours, there should be on the ship, or in its vicinity, a suitable boat ready for use for landing sick and injured persons.

28.7.2. When dockworkers are working on log booms, rafts or scows, or are stowing or unstowing a deck cargo of logs which extends above the ship's bulwark, a suitable boat, properly manned and equipped, should be moored at a suitable place.

28.8. First-aid rooms

28.8.1. (1) If as a rule 100 or more dockworkers are employed, at least one suitably equipped first-aid room should be provided at a readily accessible place for the treatment of minor injuries and as a rest place for seriously sick or injured workers.

(2) A responsible person qualified to render first aid should be in charge of the first-aid room and be readily available during working hours.

(3) The first-aid room should be under the supervision of a doctor.

28.9. Ambulance

28.9.1. (1) Arrangements should be made to ensure the prompt transport, where necessary, of sick or injured workers to a hospital or other equivalent treatment centre.

(2) Such arrangements should include facilities for promptly obtaining an ambulance carriage or launch from some place situated within a reasonable distance of the working area.

28.10. Information boards

28.10.1. Information should be conspicuously exhibited at suitable places stating—

(*a*) the position of the nearest first-aid box, first-aid room, ambulance and stretcher and the place where the person in charge can be found;

(*b*) the position of the nearest telephone for calling the ambulance, and the telephone number and name of the person or centre to be called; and

(*c*) the name, address and telephone number of the doctor to be called in an emergency.

28.11. Training in first aid

28.11.1. Dockworkers should be encouraged to become proficient in first aid.

28.11.2. (1) First-aid personnel should be adequately trained in manual resuscitation procedures and rescue work.

(2) Resuscitation apparatus, if provided, should be used only by persons trained in its use.

28.12. Register

28.12.1. (1) A first-aid register should be kept in each first-aid room for recording the names of persons to whom first aid has been rendered and the particulars of injuries and treatment.

(2) The register should be accessible only to authorised persons.

28.13. Medical examinations

28.13.1. All possible steps should be taken to ensure that all dockworkers undergo a medical examination—

(*a*) before entering employment for the first time (pre-employment examination); or when being selected or trained for the operation of mechanical equipment; and

(*b*) periodically, at such intervals as may be considered necessary by the competent authority in view of the risks inherent in the work, and the conditions under which the work is performed (periodical re-examination).

28.13.2. All medical examinations should—

(*a*) be complete and free to the workers;

(*b*) as far as is considered necessary, include X-ray and laboratory examinations.

28.13.3. In the case of workers exposed to special occupational health hazards, the periodical medical examinations should include all special investigations deemed necessary for the diagnosis of occupational diseases.

28.13.4. The data obtained by medical examinations should be suitably recorded by the medical services entrusted with carrying them out, and kept by these services for reference.

28.13.5. When the work presents a special risk to the health of a worker, he should not be employed on that work.

28.13.6. When a worker is found at the medical examination to constitute a risk of infection or a risk to the safety of other workers, he should not be allowed to work whilst the risk remains, but every effort should be made to find alternative work for him to which such risks do not attach.

28.13.7. (1) The worker should be informed of the outcome of any medical examination he has undergone.

(2) Except in the case where a dockworker requests the outcome of medical examinations to be forwarded to his own doctor, all results of medical examinations should be treated as confidential.

29. Occupational health services

29.1. General provisions

29.1.1. There should be either a special medical service for dockworkers or an occupational health service that is available to them.

29.1.2. Medical or occupational health services for, or available to, dockworkers should have the following functions:

(*a*) provision of first aid and emergency treatment;

(*b*) provision of pre-employment, periodical and special medical examinations;

(*c*) periodical training of first-aid personnel;

(*d*) surveillance of, and advice on, all conditions at workplaces and facilities that affect the health of dockworkers;

(*e*) promotion of health education among dockworkers; and

(*f*) co-operation with the competent authority in the detection, measurement and evaluation of chemical, physical or biological factors suspected of being harmful.

29.1.3. The medical service should collaborate with labour inspection (especially medical inspection) services and services concerned with treatment, job placement, accident prevention and welfare.

29.1.4. The medical service should be directed by a doctor specialising in occupational health and should be provided with an adequate staff of nurses and, if necessary, laboratory and clerical personnel.

29.1.5. Nurses employed in the medical service should possess a certificate of proficiency acceptable to the competent authority.

29.1.6. The premises occupied by the medical service should be at ground level, be conveniently accessible from all workplaces, be so designed as to allow stretcher cases to be handled easily and, so far as practicable, not be exposed to excessive noise.

29.1.7. The premises should comprise at least a waiting room, a consulting room and a treatment room, and also, if necessary, suitable accommodation for nurses and laboratory workers.

29.1.8. Rooms for waiting, consultation and treatment should—

(*a*) be sufficiently spacious, suitably lighted and ventilated, and where necessary heated; and

(*b*) have washable walls, floor and fixtures.

29.1.9. The medical service should be provided with appropriate medical and laboratory equipment and supplies and such documentation as it may require for its work.

29.1.10. The medical service should keep such records (see subparagraph 28.13.7(2)) of its activities as will provide adequate information on—

(*a*) the workers' state of health;

(*b*) the nature, circumstances and outcome of occupational injuries; and

(*c*) to the extent that such information is not provided by other agencies, the hygienic condition of workplaces, sanitary installations, etc.

30. Personnel facilities

30.1. General provisions

30.1.1. Toilet facilities, washing facilities, cloakrooms, mess rooms, canteens, hiring halls, waiting rooms and other personal service rooms should—

(*a*) be suitably situated, dimensioned, constructed, enclosed and equipped for their purpose;

(*b*) have floors, walls and ceilings that are easy to clean;

(*c*) be maintained in a clean and sanitary condition and protected against rats and other vermin; and

(*d*) be well ventilated and lighted and, if necessary, heated.

30.2. Drinking water

30.2.1. An adequate supply of cool and wholesome drinking water should be provided for and be readily accessible to all dock-workers.

30.2.2. (1) All water furnished for drinking purposes should be from a source approved by the competent health authority and controlled in the manner prescribed by this authority.

(2) Where such water is not available, the competent health authority should furnish the necessary directions for rendering the water safe for human consumption.

30.2.3. The use of common drinking cups should be prohibited.

30.2.4. Drinking water for common use should not be contained in barrels, pails, tanks or other containers from which the water must be dipped, whether they are fitted with a cover or not.

30.2.5. Where practicable, hygienic drinking fountains should be provided.

30.2.6. Where water provided for use in dock work, including fire protection, is unsuitable for drinking purposes, conspicuous notices should be posted at the points of supply stating clearly that such water is not fit to drink.

30.2.7. Points of supply of safe drinking water should be clearly marked "Drinking Water".

30.3. Toilet facilities

30.3.1. Working areas and workplaces where dock work is carried on should be provided with toilets (closets) for the maximum expected usage of the work area, separate for each sex, suitably located, as well as an adequate number of urinals.

30.3.2. (1) Where practicable, at least one closet should be available for dockworkers on board ship.

(2) Floating cranes, grain elevators, bunker machines and similar installations on or by means of which dock work is carried on should be provided with at least one closet.

30.3.3. Where practicable, closets and urinals in the interior of buildings should be of the water-flush type.

30.3.4. For personal cleansing, an adequate supply of toilet paper or, where conditions require, water should be provided.

30.3.5. Adequate washing facilities including towel and soap should be provided in or adjacent to each toilet room.

30.3.6. (1) Each closet on shore should be under cover and occupy a separate compartment which should have a separate door and be installed in a special toilet room.

(2) Each compartment door should be provided with a latch on the inside.

30.3.7. (1) Urinals should preferably consist of a row of stalls; if they are of a smaller type (cuvettes) they should be adequately separated by side partitions.

(2) Urinals should be of a suitable width.

30.3.8. A floor drain with water seal should be provided in each toilet room to facilitate flushing the floor.

30.3.9. Toilet fixtures should be constructed and maintained in conformity with good sanitary standards.

30.4. Washing facilities

30.4.1. Dock areas should be provided with sufficient and suitable washing facilities for dockworkers.

30.4.2. Washing facilities should not be used for any other purpose.

30.4.3. There should be at least one washing facility for every ten dockworkers regularly employed who have rest and meal times at the same time.

30.4.4. In wash-places—

(*a*) there should be a sufficient flow of clean water;

(*b*) there should be adequate means for removing waste water;

(*c*) suitable non-irritating soap should be provided in sufficient quantity; and

(*d*) the use of common towels should be prohibited.

30.4.5. Where dockworkers are exposed to skin contamination by poisonous, infectious or irritating substances or oil, grease or dust, at least one shower bath supplied with hot and cold water should be provided for every six workers regularly employed who are exposed to such contamination and cease work simultaneously.

30.4.6. Shower baths should be enclosed in individual compartments, with the entrance suitably screened.

30.4.7. Shower-bath equipment should be thoroughly cleaned at least once a day, and an effective disinfectant should be used to destroy fungi.

30.4.8. If dockworkers of both sexes are employed, the wash-places should be separate for each sex.

30.5. Cloakrooms

30.5.1. If as a rule 25 or more dockworkers are regularly employed at any workplace, there should be cloakrooms situated near washing facilities and equipped for the storage of the workers' working and street clothes.

30.5.2. Cloakrooms should not be used for any other purpose.

30.5.3. Cloakrooms should be provided with—

(*a*) suitable facilities for drying wet clothes;

(*b*) individual lockers, preferably of metal, with adequate ventilation, for storage of clothes; and

(*c*) benches or other suitable seating arrangements.

30.5.4. Whenever dockworkers of both sexes are employed, separate cloakrooms should be provided for each sex.

30.5.5. When women are employed and no rest room is available, some suitable space in the women's cloakroom should be provided; this space should be properly screened and suitably furnished.

30.5.6. Suitable arrangements should be made for disinfecting cloakrooms and lockers in conformity with the requirements of the competent health authority.

30.6. Mess rooms and canteens

30.6.1. If as a rule 25 or more dockworkers regularly take part in dock work on shore, or on a ship moored to the shore, a suitable room in which they can take their own meals should be provided for them unless it is possible for the workers to spend meal times in their own homes or in another suitable place which they can use free of charge.

30.6.2. Mess rooms should be provided with—

(*a*) drinking water;

(*b*) adequate facilities for washing, unless they are available in the vicinity;

(*c*) adequate facilities for cleaning utensils, table gear, etc; and

(*d*) adequate facilities for heating food and boiling water.

30.6.3. (1) Covered receptacles should be provided and used for the disposal of waste food and litter.

(2) The receptacles should be emptied after each meal and thoroughly cleaned and disinfected.

30.6.4. Where necessary, mess rooms should be available during meal and rest times to dockworkers on floating cranes, elevators, bunker machines and similar installations.

30.6.5. Mess rooms should not be used as workrooms or storage rooms.

30.6.6. Where necessary, suitable canteens for the sale and consumption of food and beverages should be provided.

30.7. Hiring halls and waiting rooms

30.7.1. Suitable hiring halls or call stands should be provided for the accommodation of dockworkers while they are being allocated for dock work.

30.7.2. Where necessary, dockworkers should be provided with suitable rooms with adequate seating accommodation in which they can wait between calls, or between the end of a call and the start of work.

31. Selection and training[1] of dockworkers

31.1. Restrictions respecting the employment of certain categories of dockworker

31.1.1. (1) No person under 18 years of age should be employed in dock work except as permitted by the competent authority and in accordance with conditions prescribed by that authority.

(2) In particular, workers under 18 but over 16 years of age may be employed for purposes of apprenticeship and training, subject to the conditions prescribed by the competent authority.

[1] See also section 28.11, which is applicable.

32. Safety and health organisation

32.1. General provisions

32.1.1. Besides ensuring that, by adequate systems of inspection or other means, regulations and instructions in regard to safety and health are observed, the competent authority should take all necessary steps to promote the co-operation of employers and dockworkers in achieving the best possible conditions of safety and health in dock work in its widest sense.

32.1.2. Safety committees on which all parties concerned are represented should be formed in each undertaking to promote safety and health activities.

32.1.3. (1) The scope of safety committees should be determined according to local circumstances.

(2) Their functions should as a rule be as follows:

(*a*) the drawing up of rules for the guidance of workers in carrying out the respective operations in a safe manner and the modification of these rules in the light of experience;

(*b*) the consideration of suggestions for improving methods of work in order to ensure greater safety and bringing these suggestions to the notice of the persons concerned so that they may be implemented;

(*c*) the consideration of reports made after the investigation of accidents; and

(*d*) the preparation of safety leaflets, posters, etc., drawing attention to particular hazards.

32.1.4. (1) Records should be kept of all accidents and cases of occupational disease affecting dockworkers.

(2) These records should be in such a form as to provide—

(*a*) the occupational accident and disease experience of each department, occupation and individual; and (*b*) the distribution of accidents by causes, with a view to facilitating preventive measures.

32.1.5. The information referred to in subparagraph 32.1.4(2) should be available to the competent authority and the safety committee.

32.1.6. Where there are a number of undertakings employing dockworkers in one and the same port, consideration should be given to the formation of a central safety organisation for the port, to which all the undertakings should affiliate.

32.1.7. The central organisation should promote occupational safety and health among dockworkers in the port by all practical methods, and in particular should stimulate and co-ordinate the activities of the safety organisations of individual undertakings.

33. Miscellaneous provisions

33.1. Reporting and investigation of occupational accidents and diseases

33.1.1. All accidents to dockworkers causing loss of life or serious personal injury should be notified forthwith to the competent authority.

33.1.2. Other injuries and occupational diseases causing incapacity for work for three days or more should be notified to the competent authority within such time and in such form as may be specified in national regulations.

33.1.3. Such accidents as may be specified in national regulations or by the competent authority (for example explosions, collapse of cranes or derricks or serious fires) should be notified forthwith to the competent authority, whether any personal injury has been caused or not.

33.1.4. The competent authority should undertake an investigation into the causes and circumstances of any accident mentioned in paragraph 33.1.1 or paragraph 33.1.3.

33.1.5. When a fatal accident has occurred, the scene of the accident should as far as practicable be left undisturbed until it has been visited by a representative of the competent authority.

33.1.6. If a dangerous failure of plant or gear has occurred, the plant or gear concerned should as far as practicable be kept available until inspected by the competent authority.

33.2. Berthing and shifting ships

33.2.1. While ships are being berthed or shifted, no work should as a rule be done by dockworkers in the holds, at the hatches or with the loading and unloading machinery and gear.

33.2.2. When ships are being moored, workers should keep clear of the mooring ropes and, in particular, should not stand in the bights of ropes being hauled by capstans.

Appendices

A. Testing of lifting appliances

A.1. General provisions

A.1.1. Every lifting appliance should be tested in accordance with the provisions of section D.1—

(*a*) before being taken into use for the first time;

(*b*) after the renewal or repair of any stress-bearing part; and

(*c*) at regular four-yearly intervals after the date on which the appliance was first taken into use.

A.1.2. The following exceptions to the requirements of paragraph A.1.1 may nevertheless be allowed:

(*a*) where any part is renewed or repaired, it should be considered sufficient to subject that part, by separate means, to the same stress as would have been imposed on it if it had been tested *in situ* during the testing of the complete appliance; and

(*b*) in the case of an appliance on board ship, the four-yearly test required under subparagraph A.1.1(*c*) may be postponed for a period not exceeding six months if such postponement would enable the test to be carried out at the same time as the four-yearly survey of the ship for classification purposes and if—

   (i) a competent person has certified in writing that in his opinion the lifting appliance may be safely operated during the period of postponement; and

   (ii) such postponement has not already taken place more than twice during the preceding 12 years and does not postpone the due date of any subsequent test, inspection or examination, which should take place as originally scheduled.

A.1.3. Every test should be carried out—

(*a*) by a competent person;

(*b*) in daylight, provided that the latitude of the place of testing so allows; otherwise, adequate lighting should be provided;

(*c*) at a time when the wind force and/or gusting does not exceed the wind force/gusting limits for which the lifting appliance was designed; and

(*d*) after all prudent precautions have been taken to ensure the safety of persons carrying out the testing and of any other person who may be in the vicinity at the time of the test.

A.2. Precautions before testing

A.2.1. Where the stability of a ship, barge or other vessel is liable to be endangered by the test unless certain precautions, such as proper ballasting, are taken, the competent person should give notice to the captain or person in charge of the vessel of the date and time of the test, the amount of test load to be applied and the maximum outreach of the lifting appliance over the side of the vessel; he should not undertake the test unless he has written confirmation from the captain or person in charge that the stability of the vessel will not be endangered by the test and that the vessel's deck and hatch covers are sufficiently strong to support the weight of the test load.

A.2.2. In the case of a gantry crane able to move on tracks along the deck, proper measures should be taken to ensure that movement of the crane along the track with the test load suspended can be safely controlled.

A.2.3. All temporary guys or stays for the mast or samson posts and, where applicable, special load-slewing guys should be rigged.

A.3. Test weights

A.3.1. (1) The weights used for making up a test weight should be suitable for the purpose and be of verified weight.

(2) All cast weights and, where practicable, other weights should be weighed on a machine of certificated accuracy; where weighing is not practicable, the weight should be determined by calculations.

(3) The weight of the test load (including the weight of its lifting

gear) should be not less than the figure determined from Appendix D nor should it exceed that figure by more than 2.5 per cent.

A.4. Derricks and derrick cranes

A.4.1. All tests should be carried out by means of test weights; except that in the case of a test following the repair or renewal of a part, a spring or hydraulic weighing machine, suitably and safely anchored, may be used; provided that this may be so rigged that the part is subjected to the calculated stress to which it would be subjected if the derrick were tested by means of dead weights as below. When a spring or hydraulic weighing machine is used, it should have an accuracy within $0 + 2.5$ per cent and the tension shall be applied for a sufficiently long period to ensure that the machine's indicator remains constant for not less than five minutes.

A.4.2. A derrick should be tested with the boom at its maximum outreach corresponding to its lowest inclination to the horizontal marked upon it or to be marked upon it in accordance with section 7.8—

(*a*) in the two extreme positions of the slewing range; and

(*b*) in the midship position.

A.4.3. In the case of a derrick crane, the boom and test load should be raised by the derrick's own winches and with the boom in one of the positions indicated in paragraph A.4.2; it should be raised by the span winch or winches as high as practicable in order that as many rope layers as possible may be reeled on the winch drum.

A.4.4. In each of the three positions indicated in paragraph A.4.2, the safe working load should be lowered at the normal lowering speed of the derrick for a distance of approximately 3 m and then braked sharply.

A.4.5. It should be demonstrated that the test load can be held stationary when the winch drive is switched off.

A.4.6. During the test it should be ascertained that, in all positions of the derrick, all parts are free to take up their appropriate positions and all ropes are running freely and are reeling up properly on the winch drums.

A.4.7. (1) Where a derrick is designed to be used in union purchase, it should be tested in union purchase with its associated derrick and rigged in accordance with the ship's rigging plan; the test load should be manœuvred throughout the working range of the union purchase and raised to such a height that the angle between the two hoist ropes is as near as practicable to 120° at some position of the working range.

(2) The test should be repeated with the derricks rigged over the opposite side of the ship.

A.4.8. Where the derrick is fitted with a span gear winch (Chapter 8), it should be tested with the derrick it serves and each sprocket should be subjected to load.

A.4.9. Upon completion of tests with the test load, each winch should be tested with its safe working load suspended and the derrick placed in various positions, such that each winch serving the derrick is subjected to loading whilst having the maximum working length of rope layered upon its drum.

A.5. Cranes

A.5.1. (1) Test weights only should be employed.

(2) Before any test is carried out, it should be ascertained, from the manufacturer's rating or known design limitations, that the crane has been designed to withstand the imposition of the test load not only as regards its structural strength but also as regards its stability where this is appropriate. In the absence of manufacturer's ratings or known design information, the design features should be appraised by a competent person.

(3) It should be ascertained—not merely assumed—that where appropriate the crane is properly ballasted.

(4) Only a competent driver should be employed during the test.

(5) A mobile crane should be on level ground that is sufficiently firm to ensure that indentation or subsidence does not take place; its outriggers (if provided) should be properly fitted and where necessary should be resting on timber baulks or similar supports.

(6) Tracks and rails should be checked for soundness.

(7) Tyre pressures (where applicable) should be correct.

(8) The automatic safe load indicator (section 5.7) should, if of a type liable to be damaged by the extent of the test loading, be disconnected.

(9) When a crane is tested in the "free on wheels" condition, the axle springs or absorbers should be chocked or locked.

(10) The radius at which the test load should be applied should be measured in accordance with section 4.13.

(11) In every case, the test load should be raised sufficiently to subject every tooth in the gear wheels to loading.

(12) A test load should not be deposited upon soft muddy ground.[1]

(13) Where a crane is secured to the structure of a building, the test should not be carried out until the owner of the building has confirmed in writing that the structure is sufficiently strong to withstand the extra strain imposed upon it during the test.

A.5.2. When gantry traveller cranes, transporters and similar lifting appliances are tested, the crane should be positioned approximately midway between any two gantry track supports; the test load should be lifted just clear of the ground and slowly traversed from one end of the bridge span to the other. In the case of a transporter, the crab or trolley supporting the test load should be slowly traversed along the whole length of the track; in the case of a gantry crane on board ship, the test load should be slowly traversed along the whole length of the track—

---

[1] Because when the load is lifted again, the momentary extra resistance caused by suction between the load and the ground may be a source of danger.

(*a*) with the test load as far as practicable on one side; and

(*b*) with the test load as far as practicable on the other side.

A.5.3. (1) When a mobile crane is tested, no overload test should be carried out before it has been ascertained that the crane has a sufficient margin of stability. A stability test on the crane should have been carried out by the manufacturer or, in the case of a series-produced crane, on the prototype model of that crane.

(2) When any other crane is tested, such as a derrick crane that either has rigid back-stays anchored to the ground or is ballasted, an anchoring or ballast test should be carried out if the safety of the anchoring or ballasting is in doubt or after it has been erected. The amount of test load and the manner of its application should be indicated by the manufacturer or be determined by a competent person, and should be applied with the jib or boom in a position where—

(*a*) the maximum pull on the anchorage or ballasting is achieved; or

(*b*) a reduced load at an increased radius gives an equivalent pull.

(3) When a crane has a jib or boom of variable length, the test indicated in subparagraph (2) should be conducted with the jib or boom at its maximum length, at its minimum length, and at a length approximately midway between the maximum and minimum lengths.

(4) When a boom is fitted with a fly jib or provided with more than one fly jib of different lengths, the test should be conducted on the shortest fly jib in combination with the main boom length that gives the greatest rated load on the fly jib; the test should also be conducted on the longest fly jib in combination with the main boom length that gives the greatest rated load on the fly jib. A further test should be conducted on the longest possible combination of main and fly jibs. Before these tests are carried out, the manufacturer's table of safe working loads for all combinations of boom length and fly jib or jibs should be made available to the competent person conducting the tests. The tests should be carried out at the position of least stability as defined by the manufacturer.

(5) Where the safe working load of a crane varies according to whether it is used with stabilising spreaders or "free on wheels", the above tests, as appropriate, should be carried out for each condition.

(6) After the load test, the crane should be put through all its motions at their maximum rated speeds with the safe working load suspended (except where the crane can freely slew through 360°, in which case slewing should be restricted to not more than two complete turns from start to stop). All brakes should be tested.

(7) Tests should also be carried out with the jib or boom at such an angle of rotation and elevation as to create the conditions of least stability as defined by the manufacturer or a competent person.

A.5.4. After the overload test, the automatic safe load indicators should be reconnected and tested by progressively applying a load to the crane until the visual and audible warnings operate. The load should be lowered to the ground on each occasion that an increment of load is applied, and then hoisted.[1]

A.5.5. All limit switches should be tested to ascertain that they are functioning correctly.

A.5.6. Upon completion of the test, the lifting appliance should be thoroughly examined by the competent person in accordance with Appendix C.

---

[1] Because otherwise the hysteris effect in the crane's structure may cause unreliable readings.

B. Testing of loose gear

B.1. General provisions

B.1.1. (1) Every item of loose gear, other than a cargo block, should be tested in accordance with the provisions of section D.3.

(2) Every cargo block should be tested in accordance with the provisions of section D.2.

B.1.2. Every item of loose gear, including cargo blocks, lifting beams and lifting frames, should be tested—

(*a*) before it is taken into service for the first time; and

(*b*) after any renewal or repair of a stress-bearing part.

B.2. Physical testing equipment

B.2.1. (1) Recording test equipment used in carrying out overload proof tests, either of assembled units or of loose gear components, should have been tested for accuracy by a competent person at least once during the 12 months preceding the test.

(2) Such test should be performed with equipment that meets the standards set by the national authority, or any such appropriate standard as has been verified as meeting the requirements of a national authority or other standard.

(3) Machine errors should be taken into account in conducting tests.

(4) A copy of the test reports should be displayed.

(5) The characteristics and capacity of the recording test equipment used should be suitable for the proof tests performed.

B.2.2. Where the safe working load of the loose gear is so high or is of such a size that a testing machine is not available for applying the proof test load, or where it is not practicable to do so, the test may be carried out by suspending it from a suitable structure or lifting appliance and applying test weights. The weights should comply with the requirements of section A.3.

B.2.3. The test load on a spreader beam or frame should be so applied that it will impose the maximum stress in the beam; all fittings such as hooks, rings and chain should be tested independently before being fitted to the beam.

B.2.4. A pulley block should, whenever possible, be tested with its sheaves reeved, the end of the rope being properly anchored to the becket of the block. Where this is not practicable, the becket should be tested independently.

B.2.5. Slings with crate clamps, barrel hooks, plate clamps or other similar devices should be tested as nearly as possible in the manner in which they are used, i.e. at the angle at which the clamp or other device is designed to be used. The clamp or other device should be applied to a baulk of timber or special steel jig such that its holding or gripping strength is tested.

C. Thorough examination and inspection of lifting appliances and loose gear

C.1. General provisions

C.1.1. (1) For the purpose of this appendix thorough examination is defined as a detailed visual examination supplemented, where considered necessary by the competent person, by such other means as non-destructive testing, carried out as carefully as the conditions permit in order to arrive at a reliable conclusion as to the safety of the appliance or gear examined.

(2) Where the competent person considers it necessary, parts of the lifting appliance or loose gear should be dismantled by a skilled person to the extent required by the competent person.

(3) In the case of ship's gear, the examination should include associated ship's fittings such as deck eyes, mast bands, temporary stays and cleats.

C.1.2. (1) For the purpose of this appendix inspection is defined as a visual survey carried out by a competent person as carefully as the conditions permit in order to determine whether any part of the lifting appliance or the gear has any readily detectable deformation, distortion, malfunctioning, wear, corrosion or any other visible defect liable to affect the continued safety of the appliance or gear.

(2) Where the competent person considers it necessary, any parts of a lifting appliance or loose gear that may be dismantled reasonably readily should be so dismantled.

C.1.3. For the purpose of this appendix a competent person is defined as a person who—

(*a*) has sufficient practical and theoretical knowledge and experience of the appliance or gear he examines to assess its safety and continued fitness for use;

(*b*) knows how the appliance or gear he examines should be prepared for examination or inspection, as the case may be;

(*c*) has sufficient practical and theoretical knowledge and experience of any equipment he uses to test and/or thoroughly examine the appliance or gear; and

(*d*) has been approved as qualified in his field.

C.1.4. (1) No lifting appliance should be used unless it has been thoroughly examined—

(*a*) after every test carried out in accordance with paragraph A.1.1;

(*b*) in the case of a lifting appliance other than a ship's derrick (but including a ship's derrick crane), after placing it in service, at least once during the preceding 12 months; or

(*c*) in the case of a ship's cargo lift, at least once during the preceding six months.

(2) No lifting appliance should be used unless any wire rope forming part of it has been thoroughly examined—

(*a*) where the rope does not pass over a sheave or winding drum, during the preceding 12 months; or

(*b*) where the rope does pass over a sheave or winding drum, during the preceding six months.

(3) No ship's derrick should be used unless it has been inspected by a competent person at least once during the preceding 12 months.

C.1.5. (1) No loose gear should be used unless it has been thoroughly examined—

(*a*) after every test carried out in accordance with section B.1;

(*b*) after placing in service, at least once during the preceding six months.

(2) No bridle, sling, chain, chain sling or other piece of loose gear should be used in any cargo-handling operation unless it has been inspected by a competent person since the last job for which the gear was issued.

C.1.6. Every part of a lifting appliance or gear specified by the competent person should be properly cleaned and prepared before the examination or inspection.

D. Test loading

D.1. Lifting appliances

D.1.1. The test load applied to a lifting appliance should exceed the safe working load (SWL) of the appliance as follows:

SWL (*tonnes*)	*Test load* (*tonnes*)
Up to 20	25 per cent greater than SWL
21–50	5 tonnes greater than SWL
51 and above	10 per cent greater than SWL

D.2. Cargo or pulley blocks

D.2.1. The test load applied to a cargo or pulley block should exceed the SWL of the block as follows:

SWL (*tonnes*)	*Test load* (*tonnes*)
Single-sheave block:	
All safe working loads	$4 \times$ SWL
Multi-sheave block:	
Up to 25	$2 \times$ SWL
26–160	$(0.933 \times \text{SWL}) + 27$
161 and above	$1.1 \times$ SWL

D.3. Loose gear

D.3.1. The test load applied to an item of loose gear should exceed the SWL of the gear as follows:

SWL (*tonnes*)	*Test load* (*tonnes*)
Chain, hook, shackle, ring, link, clamp and similar gear:	
Up to 25	$2 \times SWL$
26 and above	$(1.22 \times SWL) + 20$
Lifting beam, lifting frame and similar gear:	
Up to 10	$2 \times SWL$
11–160	$(1.04 \times SWL) + 9.6$
161 and above	$1.1 \times SWL$

E. Coefficient of utilisation (factor of safety)

E.1. Wire rope[1]

E.1.1. For a wire rope used in the construction of a sling or forming part of a derrick, derrick crane or crane on board ship, the coefficient of utilisation should be—

(*a*) in the case of a wire rope having a safe working load (SWL) of up to 160 tonnes, not less than

$$\frac{10^4}{(8.85 \times \text{SWL}) + 1910}\text{; or}$$

(*b*) 3, in the case of a wire rope having a SWL of 161 tonnes and above.

E.1.2. For a wire rope forming part of a crane other than on board ship, the coefficient of utilisation should be—

(*a*) calculated according to the formula given in subparagraph E.1.1(*a*); or

(*b*) as given in a recognised national or international standard to which the appliance has been designed and constructed.

E.1.3. These coefficients should be adopted unless other requirements are laid down in a recognised national or international standard.

E.2. Fibre rope[2]

E.2.1. For a fibre rope (man-made or natural), the coefficient of utilisation should be related to the diameter of the rope, as follows:

Diameter of rope (mm)	12	14–17	18–23	24–39	40 and above
Coefficient	12	10	8	7	6

E 2.2. These coefficients should be adopted unless other requirements are laid down in a recognised national or international standard.

---

1 See section 9.2.

2 See section 10.2.

F. Steel quality grade mark

F.1.1. The quality grade mark to be placed on any steel component of loose gear in accordance with paragraph 20.6 should be as follows:

Quality grade mark	Grade of steel	Mean stress in a piece of chain made up in accordance with the appropriate ISO standard of the material at the breaking load specified in the standard
L	Mild	300 N/mm^2
M	Higher tensile	400 ,,
P	Alloy	500 ,,
S	Alloy	630 ,,
T	Alloy	800 ,,

G. Heat treatment of wrought iron

G.1. General provisions

G.1.1. Heat treatment of wrought-iron gear should consist of heating the gear uniformly in a suitably constructed muffle furnace until the whole of the metal has attained a temperature between 600°C (1,100°F) and 650°C (1,200°F), then withdrawing the gear from the furnace and allowing it to cool uniformly.

G.1.2. If the past history of wrought-iron gear is not known or if it is suspected that the gear has been heat-treated at an incorrect temperature, before putting it to work it should be given normalising treatment (950°C–1,000°C or 1,750°F–1,830°F) followed by uniform cooling, precautions being taken during the heat treatment to prevent excessive scaling.

G.1.3. (1) Sling assemblies should be made of materials having similar properties.

(2) When, however, the assembly has some components of wrought iron and others of mild steel (e.g. mild-steel hooks permanently connected to wrought-iron chains), it should be normalised at a temperature between 920°C and 950°C (1,700°F and 1,750°F), removed from the furnace and cooled uniformly.

H. Marking of single-sheave blocks

H.1. General provisions

H.1.1. This appendix explains the method of marking the safe working load (SWL) of a single-sheave block in a derrick rig. For the sake of simplicity the effect of friction and rope stiffness (i.e. the effort required to bend the rope round the sheave) has been ignored. In practice the assessment of the SWL of the block as in paragraph H.2.2 does, in fact, ignore friction and rope stiffness; these factors should nevertheless be taken into account when determining the resultant force on the head fittings of heel blocks, span gear blocks and other equipment. This is the responsibility of the competent person who prepares the ship's rigging plan.

H.2. Method

H.2.1. A single-sheave block may be rigged at various positions in the derrick rig, as for example in the span gear, upper and lower cargo blocks or heel blocks; it may be used with or without a becket.

H.2.2. The SWL of a single-sheave block is always assessed in accordance with one fundamental condition of loading, i.e. the particular case where the block is suspended by its head fitting and the dead weight or cargo load is attached to a wire rope passing round the sheave in such a way that the hauling part is parallel to the part to which the load is attached (see figure 1). *The SWL marked on the block is the dead weight* (M *tonnes*) *that can safely be lifted by the block when rigged in this way.*

H.2.3. When the block is rigged as in paragraph H.2.2, the resultant force on the head fitting is twice the SWL marked on the block (i.e. $2M$ tonnes). The block manufacturer should design the block in such a way that the head fitting, axle pin and strop are capable of safely withstanding the resultant force of $2M$ tonnes. Consequently a proof load of twice the designed SWL (i.e. $4M$ tonnes) should be applied to the block.

H.2.4. When the block is rigged as a lower cargo block, i.e. when the dead weight or cargo load is secured directly to the head fitting (with the block therefore being upside down) instead of to the rope passing round the sheave (see figure 2), the SWL marked on the block is unchanged. The resultant force or load now acting on the head fitting is only M tonnes. However, as the block has been designed to withstand safely a resultant force on the head fitting of $2M$ tonnes, it follows that the block is safe to lift a dead weight or cargo load of $2M$ which gives the same stresses in the block as when it is rigged as in figure 1. Normally, however, national regulations prohibit the use of a lifting device to lift a load in excess of the SWL marked on it, and in all but this particular case this is the correct procedure. In this particular case, and only in this case, the regulations should allow that a single-sheave block may lift twice the SWL marked on it when rigged as in figure 2 only.

H.2.5. When a suitable size of single-sheave block is to be selected for use elsewhere in the rig (for example, in a mast head span block or a derrick heel block), the maximum resultant force on the head fitting arising from the tension in the span rope should first be determined (see figure 3). This force can be obtained from the rigging plan (see section 7.1). The value of this resultant force varies according to the angle of the derrick boom to the horizontal, so that the rigging plan should show the maximum value. If this resultant force is represented by R tonnes, the correct block to be used at this position would be one marked with a SWL equal to one-half of the resultant force (i.e. $\frac{R}{2}$ tonnes). It is extremely important to note, however, that the shackle and link used to attach this block to the mast eye *should have and be marked with a SWL equal to* R *tonnes.* This applies, of course, to all shackled and links used for connecting blocks elsewhere in the derrick rig.

H.2.6. In the case of the rig shown in figure 4 (sometimes termed the gun-tackle rig), actual figures will serve best to explain the principle of application. Suppose the derrick is marked "SWL 4 tonnes", which is the dead weight or cargo load that can be safely

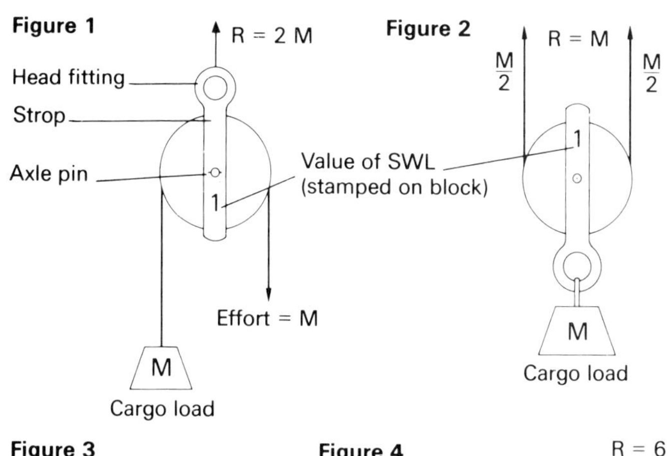
Figure 1
R = 2 M
Head fitting
Strop
Axle pin
1
Value of SWL
(stamped on block)
Effort = M
M
Cargo load
Figure 2
R = M
M/2
M/2
1
M
Cargo load

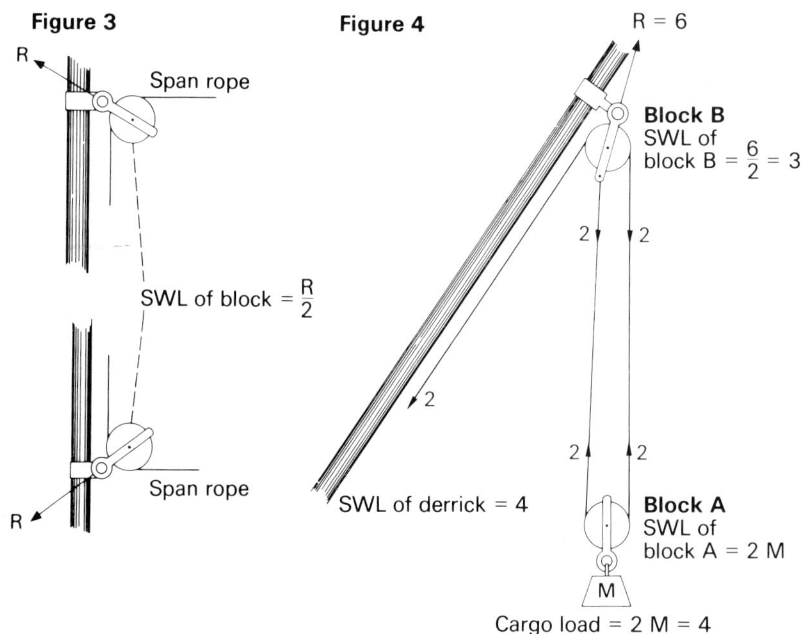
Figure 3
R
Span rope
SWL of block = R/2
Span rope
R
Figure 4
R = 6
Block B
SWL of
block B = 6/2 = 3
2
2
2
2
2
SWL of derrick = 4
Block A
SWL of
block A = 2 M
M
Cargo load = 2 M = 4

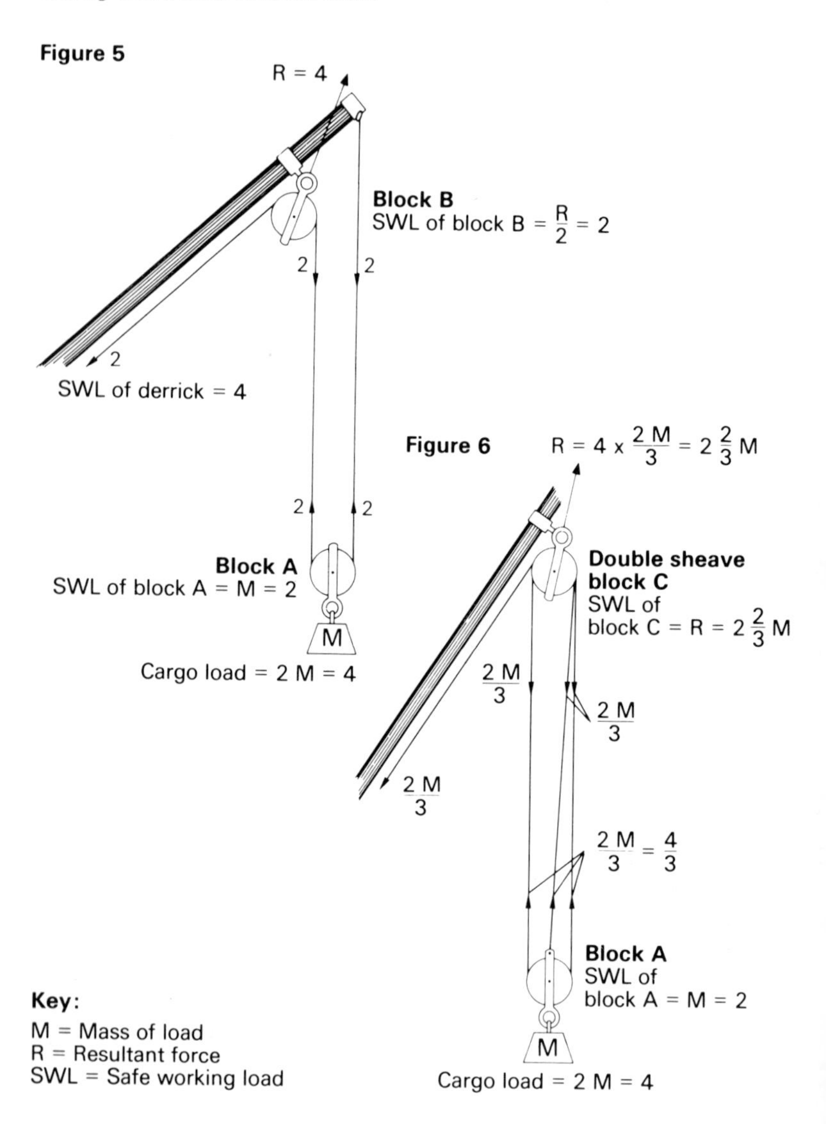
Figure 5
R = 4
Block B
SWL of block B = $\frac{R}{2}$ = 2
2
2
2
SWL of derrick = 4
2
2
Block A
SWL of block A = M = 2
M
Cargo load = 2 M = 4
Figure 6
R = 4 x $\frac{2M}{3}$ = 2 $\frac{2}{3}$ M
Double sheave block C
SWL of block C = R = 2 $\frac{2}{3}$ M
$\frac{2M}{3}$
$\frac{2M}{3}$
$\frac{2M}{3}$
$\frac{2M}{3} = \frac{4}{3}$
Block A
SWL of block A = M = 2
M
Cargo load = 2 M = 4
Key:
M = Mass of load
R = Resultant force
SWL = Safe working load

handled by the derrick as a whole. It follows from paragraph H.2.4 that the lower cargo block A will be marked with a SWL of 2 tonnes but is permitted to support a cargo load of 4 tonnes. The upper block B will have a resultant force on its head fitting of 6 tonnes,[1] so that the SWL of the block selected for fitting here would be $\frac{R}{2}$ (i.e. $\frac{6}{2}$ or 3 tonnes). For the purpose of these examples the fact that all the wires are not parallel has been ignored, although in practice this would not be so and the true resultant would be shown on the rigging plan.

H.2.7. Another common single-sheave block rig is shown in figure 5. The lower cargo block A would, as before, have a SWL of 2 tonnes marked on it, since this is another case where the load is directly attached to the head of the block, thus making it subject to the dispensation allowed under paragraph H.2.4, i.e. a cargo load of 4 tonnes could be lifted. The block in position B would, as explained in paragraph H.2.5, be one having a SWL of one-half the resultant force R marked on it.

H.2.8. The rig shown in figure 6 incorporates a single-sheave block fitted with a becket. The upper block B will in this case be a multi-sheave block and should therefore be dealt with in accordance with section 6.2. The lower block is a single-sheave block fitted with a becket. The cargo load is attached directly to it and the dispensation allowed under paragraph H.2.4 applies to it, i.e. it is stamped M tonnes but can lift $2M$ tonnes. The only effect of the becket as far as the lower single-sheave block is concerned is to reduce the tension in the wire rope from M to $\frac{2M}{3}$ tonnes (i.e. from 2 to $1\frac{1}{3}$ tonnes). If this were a permanent rig, a smaller size of rope would clearly be used. *The SWL of a single-sheave block fitted with a becket is assessed in the same way as other single-sheave blocks, i.e. according to paragraph H.2.2.*

---

[1] See, however, paragraph H.1.1.

Index